In Our Own Words

Stories of Young AAs in Recovery

from the pages of the AA Grapevine

Other Books Published by AA Grapevine, Inc.
The Language of the Heart
The Best of the Grapevine, Volume 1
The Best of the Grapevine, Volume 2
The Best of the Grapevine, Volume 3
AA Around the World
The Best of Bill
Thank You for Sharing
Spiritual Awakenings
I Am Responsible: The Hand of AA
The Home Group: Heartbeat of AA
Emotional Sobriety — The Next Frontier

In Spanish:
El Lenguaje del Corazón
Lo Mejor de Bill
El Grupo Base: corazón de AA

In French:
Le langage du cœur
Les meilleurs articles de Bill
Le groupe d'attache : Le battement du cœur des AA

In Our Own Words

Stories of Young AAs in Recovery

From the pages of the AA Grapevine

AA Grapevine, Inc.
New York, New York
www.aagrapevine.org

AA Preamble

Alcoholics Anonymous is a fellowship of men and women who share their experience, strength and hope with each other that they may solve their common problem and help others to recover from alcoholism.

The only requirement for membership is a desire to stop drinking. There are no dues or fees for AA membership; we are self-supporting through our own contributions.

AA is not allied with any sect, denomination, politics, organization or institution; does not wish to engage in any controversy, neither endorses nor opposes any causes. Our primary purpose is to stay sober and help other alcoholics to achieve sobriety.

The Twelve Steps of Alcoholics Anonymous

1. We admitted we were powerless over alcohol — that our lives had become unmanageable.
2. Came to believe that a Power greater than ourselves could restore us to sanity.
3. Made a decision to turn our will and our lives over to the care of God as we understood Him.
4. Made a searching and fearless moral inventory of ourselves.
5. Admitted to God, to ourselves and to another human being the exact nature of our wrongs.
6. Were entirely ready to have God remove all these defects of character.
7. Humbly asked Him to remove our shortcomings.
8. Made a list of all persons we had harmed and became willing to make amends to them all.
9. Made direct amends to such people wherever possible, except when to do so would injure them or others.
10. Continued to take personal inventory and when we were wrong promptly admitted it.
11. Sought through prayer and meditation to improve our conscious contact with God, as we understood Him, praying only for knowledge of His will for us and the power to carry that out.
12. Having had a spiritual awakening as the result of these steps, we tried to carry this message to alcoholics, and to practice these principles in all our affairs.

The Twelve Traditions of Alcoholics Anonymous

1. Our common welfare should come first; personal recovery depends upon A.A. unity.
2. For our group purpose there is but one ultimate authority — a loving God as He may express Himself in our group conscience. Our leaders are but trusted servants; they do not govern.
3. The only requirement for A.A. membership is a desire to stop drinking.
4. Each group should be autonomous except in matters affecting other groups or A.A. as a whole.
5. Each group has but one primary purpose — to carry its message to the alcoholic who still suffers.
6. An A.A. group ought never endorse, finance, or lend the A.A. name to any related facility or outside enterprise, lest problems of money, property, and prestige divert us from our primary purpose.
7. Every A.A. group ought to be fully self-supporting, declining outside contributions.
8. Alcoholics Anonymous should remain forever nonprofessional, but our service centers may employ special workers.
9. A.A., as such, ought never be organized; but we may create service boards or committees directly responsible to those they serve.
10. Alcoholics Anonymous has no opinion on outside issues; hence the A.A. name ought never be drawn into public controversy.
11. Our public relations policy is based on attraction rather than promotion; we need always maintain personal anonymity at the level of press, radio, and films.
12. Anonymity is the spiritual foundation of all our traditions, ever reminding us to place principles before personalities.

Alcoholics Anonymous

AA's program of recovery is fully set forth in its basic text, *Alcoholics Anonymous* (commonly known as the Big Book), now in its Fourth Edition, as well as in *Twelve Steps and Twelve Traditions* and other books. Information on AA can also be found on AA's website at www.aa.org, or by writing to: Alcoholics Anonymous, Box 459, Grand Central Station, New York, NY 10163. For local resources, check your local telephone directory under "Alcoholics Anonymous." Two pamphlets, "Too Young?" and "Young People and A.A." are also available from AA.

The AA Grapevine

The Grapevine is AA's international monthly journal, published continuously since its first issue in June 1944. The AA pamphlet on the Grapevine describes its scope and purpose this way: "As an integral part of Alcoholics Anonymous for more than sixty years, the Grapevine publishes articles that reflect the full diversity of experience and thought found within the AA fellowship. No one viewpoint or philosophy dominates its pages, and in determining content, the editorial staff relies on the principles of the Twelve Traditions."

In addition to a monthly magazine, the Grapevine also produces anthologies, audiobooks, and CDs based on published articles, an annual wall calendar, and a pocket planner. The entire collection of Grapevine articles is available online in its Digital Archive. AudioGrapevine, the magazine in digital audio format, is available as well. AA Grapevine also publishes La Viña, AA's Spanish-language magazine.

For more information on the Grapevine, or to subscribe, please visit the magazine's website at www.aagrapevine.org or write to:

The AA Grapevine
475 Riverside Drive
New York, NY 10115

You may also call: 1-800-631-6025 (US)
1-815-734-5856 (International)

E-mail: customerservice@aagrapevine.org

Table of Contents

Section Six: **FRIENDS WE HAVEN'T MET YET:**
Working and Playing with Others

Section Seven: **HAPPY, JOYOUS, AND REAL**

Foreword

Getting sober and staying sober isn't easy at any age. But its starting place is clearly marked: "Recovery begins when one alcoholic talks with another alcoholic, sharing experience, strength, and hope," says one foreword to the book *Alcoholics Anonymous*. It begins with stories like the ones in this book.

Most of us alcoholics are convinced that we are different, that we are too young or too old, too smart or too savvy to have a problem with drinking; we couldn't possibly be drunks. But, after hearing other people's stories, we discover that no one is immune to suffering. Others have felt the same soul-searing pain that we have. Others have felt just as desperate, angry, and afraid. After listening to AA members' stories, we realize that other people understand us. We are not alone. People like us recover. We begin to have hope.

That is what you can find in this volume. A collection of stories by AA members who got sober in their teens, twenties, and early thirties, *In Our Own Words* not only articulates some of the difficulties faced by alcoholics young in years, but also describes some of the sober joys that await.

The stories in Section One are candid accounts of the drinking lives of ten young alcoholics. Some, like "Wanted" and "Far from Innocent," depict the dark places that drinking took the writers. Others, like "Ten Minutes of Oneness," capture the emotional and spiritual ravages that many alcoholics endure.

The stories in Sections Two through Four point to a way out. Talking about how they managed to get and stay sober, the writers describe what happens in meetings, how others have helped them, and the impact that practicing the principles of AA has had on their lives. In Sections Five through Seven, the stories describe what life in recovery can be like. In "Family Connections," writers reflect on the unexpected ways AA can heal families; in "Friends We Haven't Met Yet," AAs discover the unexpected pleasures of helping others; and in "Happy, Joyous, and Real," they describe the challenges and rewards of finally learning to live and love, one day at a time.

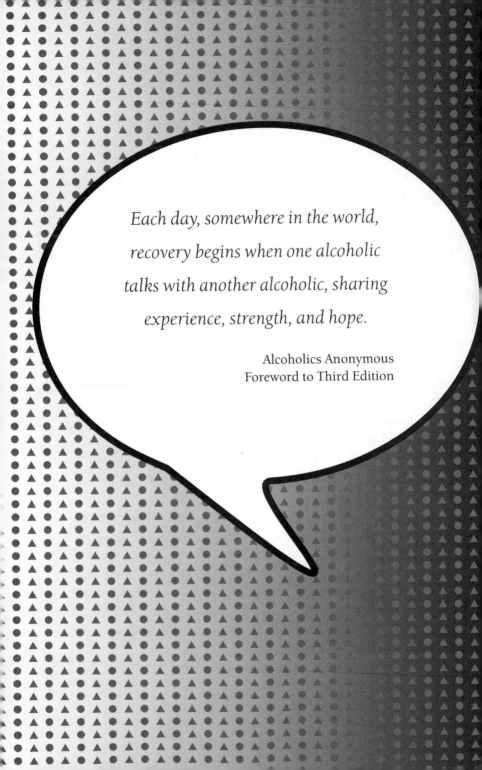

*Each day, somewhere in the world,
recovery begins when one alcoholic
talks with another alcoholic, sharing
experience, strength, and hope.*

Alcoholics Anonymous
Foreword to Third Edition

Section One: **WHAT WE USED TO BE LIKE**

Haven't You Had Enough?

AS I SAT IN MY CHAIR and looked around the room, I thought to myself that there was no way I belonged with these people. So what if I drank a little more than my friends? An alcoholic I was not. I was too young.

I started drinking at the age of eleven. When I drank, I became funny and beautiful, and it seemed to me I had friends. But somewhere along the way I crossed an invisible line. And drinking was no longer something I could choose. My friends had begun to say, "Haven't you had enough?" But as drunk as I was, I had just started.

My self-esteem vanished. I was no one. Only when a guy said I was beautiful, did I even think, "Maybe I'm alright."

I hated the sight of what I'd become. I started to isolate. I became suicidal. My parents, not knowing that I was drinking, didn't know what to do with a depressed teenager.

Then I found tequila, and during my last year of drinking, I never drew a sober breath. I drank to the point of no friends and no self-worth. No one could trust me, not even my parents. The next day, I was in a thirty-day treatment program. That day, sobriety began. It was March 21, 1988. I was thirteen years old.

Today, I know who I am. Very proudly in my meetings I announce that I am an alcoholic. I pray daily, even just to ask my Higher Power (whom I choose to call God) to walk with me that day. He has never left me, even when I have left him. I'm active in AA — shaking hands, chairing meetings, making coffee, reading, and sharing my experience, strength, and hope. I try to live the Twelve Steps of AA. I've found that they apply to my every situation in life since I still have to learn to live life on life's terms.

Every one of us in AA is a miracle. The gratitude I have is just to be breathing today... I was so close to dying. And although I have a lot of "yets" out there, I have true friends who love me. All I need to do is call them and go to meetings, work my program, and for today the "yets" won't come.

So I write this to thank all of you for keeping the AA program strong and giving me a chance to continue my sobriety today.

A. C.
Raleigh, North Carolina
August 1999

Staying in the Momentum

I HAD MY FIRST DRINK when I was eleven years old, and it was wonderful. The first drink did so much for me that I had to have another and another. I was drunk and felt incredible. Up to that point in my life, I'd always been discontented with things, and now I had found the cure. Alcohol made me feel big, important, and content with life. I could feel the alcohol going through my veins, warming the chilly emptiness I always felt.

I started drinking on the weekends whenever I could get the stuff. Not many people wanted to have anything to do with alcohol in middle school, yet by the time I got to high school a lot of people joined in. But I gradually became aware that not everyone drank the way I did. The only thing I could think about was drinking: how much I needed and whom I would drink with. During the week, I was full of anger and stress, so when Friday arrived, I was ready. Others seemed able to get by with or without alcohol, but I had to have it. I couldn't understand how people could just drink a couple and stop. Putting alcohol into my body was like giving me energy. I came alive.

During high school, I had troubles with the police and with my family. I would be asked, "Do you think you have a problem with alcohol?" And I would quickly say, "No." The only thing that ran through my mind was what life would be like without the alcohol. I can remember being scared to

3

pick up a date, and how a few drinks before I arrived seemed to help.

By this time there were some people I didn't enjoy drinking around because they wouldn't do it the way I did. I began to feel withdrawn the day after drinking. I usually woke up still tipsy, and as that wore off, I became jittery and befogged.

When I was eighteen, I enrolled in college — and found paradise. College will hide a drunk. The only thing on my mind was drinking and rushing a fraternity. The routine was pretty predictable. If I started drinking during the week, I'd drink every day until Sunday night. Sunday nights were when my fraternity held its meetings, plus I had to get in shape for the upcoming week. Usually I could make it until Tuesday before I started again. The worst was experiencing Sunday and Monday without any alcohol. I began to have breathing problems and would wake up thinking my heart had stopped. I was shaking all the time and sweating all over the place. But when I began to drink, the shaking calmed and the breathing problem stopped.

On mornings after drinking, I felt an incredible fear and emptiness. I remember listening to my mother and father on the answering machine and not picking up the receiver because I didn't want them to know I was in pain. I couldn't make it to any classes and the responsibilities that I had weren't being attended to. This was always on my mind and I felt pretty useless. As soon as I started to drink, all these things fell from my shoulders and I was free. I'd be studying and the thought of drinking and the "good feeling" would pop into my mind. Drinking would usually win out, and off I would go. I never thought about the emptiness, fear, shaking, or withdrawal; I could only think of the escape and freedom.

Some mornings I told myself, "Not tonight. Just rest — you need it." I told myself, "This has got to stop." Yet I couldn't say no.

I couldn't understand how people could do things like play ball before they went out, go hiking on Saturdays, go to the movies, or decide to "take it easy tonight." I couldn't understand why people left a tailgate to actually go see the football game.

One semester I was dating this girl and she broke up with me. The emptiness and fear grew to an amazing extreme. I'd been drunk for about a week prior to this and stayed drunk for another week. But alcohol wasn't freeing me anymore. I was in emotional turmoil, failing at school, and felt like I was going to collapse to the ground and go into convulsions.

I'd known for two years that I had a drinking problem, but I just couldn't picture my life without the alcohol. Then on February 15, 1992, I was asked once again if I thought I had a problem. This time I said yes and asked for help.

To be honest I really only intended to clean up for a month or so in order to get myself out of the jam I was in and to dry out. When I came into AA, I thought I was different. Then an AA member who was committed to carrying the message came over and told me what it had been like for him. Wow! He had thought and drank the same way I did. I was sold.

Once I started to feel better and to accumulate some time, I started to question whether or not I was an alcoholic. I'd listen to the stories at speaker meetings and would compare myself out. I hadn't lost a wife or my family, hadn't had a heart attack, never beat my kids, never spent a year in jail, didn't have blackouts every time I drank. And by golly, I wasn't fifty-five years old!

I was resentful of the people in the meetings who were living life happily without alcohol. I was extremely angry much of the time. I can remember punching walls and having intense arguments.

I'm eternally grateful to a person who took me aside one day and sat me down in front of the Big Book. He talked and I listened. He pointed out the "Doctor's Opinion," "There Is a Solution," and "More About Alcoholism," then finished with the first paragraph of "We Agnostics." It is in these chapters that the disease of alcoholism is talked about in great detail. I'd been in AA for over a year and I didn't even know what an alcoholic really was. I knew that my life was unmanageable because of my drinking, but that was all. I saw that I had three choices: work the program on a daily basis as it was intended, drink, or go insane.

I've been given the chance to have choices and live life. I couldn't have dreamed of having the life I do now. The Big Book is a text and I read it every day. I go to lots of meetings. I get there early and help set up. I stay late and help clean up. I extend my hand as it was extended to me. I hit my knees in the morning and at night. I clean house daily. I use my sponsor. I do the best I can to give away what has been so freely given to me. I've been given a second chance and I'm here to be of service.

Action is the key because "self" wants to creep in; "self" is what holds me back today. I must do these actions no matter how I feel or how my day went: had a great day, do the actions; had a bad day, do the actions. These actions keep the momentum going so when tough times come I'm on auto pilot. I give thanks to AA and a power greater than myself for the gift of sobriety today.

Scot G.
Blacksburg, Virginia
August 1995

I've Never Had a Legal Drink

I WAS BROUGHT UP in an alcoholic, dysfunctional home—dysfunctional mostly because I was in it. My father was an active AA member, but in the twenty years he was "on" the program, he never put a year of continuous sobriety together. My mother was a functioning alcoholic who drank every night in the solitude of her bedroom. I lived in a house of fear.

My mother told me if I ever found my dad's booze to "get rid of it." So when I found it, I got rid of it: I drank it.

My first drink was on a resentment; at my father for abandoning me every time he chose booze over me, at my mom for making me responsible to fix my dad, at the booze for being so much more important than me, and at God for putting me in this family.

I immediately found out why both of my parents chose booze over reality. I was an instant alcoholic. I drank to oblivion.

My dad sensed the change in me and began promoting AA to me with incentives such as "Hey, there are some young, cute guys in the Fellowship." Well, my dad was right — those young, cute guys were there. I was able to see that even though AA wasn't working for my dad, it did work. People were actually staying sober for more than a year. I attended meetings for ninety days, then I got back into life and busy again. I put together a year and a half of not drinking, without the program, and I chose to go back out.

It took only a year for me to find my way back in AA, utterly defeated. This time I got a sponsor who was eighteen and had five years of sobriety (not uncommon). I attended meetings regularly and began to build a spiritual foundation with my Higher Power. I can also utilize my religious teachings, but I always remember that "religion is for people who are afraid of hell, and spirituality is for people who have been there."

God has blessed me with the precious gift of sobriety. He has never given me more than I can handle. He has put everything in my life that is good. God is my center of being. Nothing on this earth matters except for my spiritual growth. I have found that God is in me, in you, in all. He has given me the gifts of intuition, intelligence, and love. I don't live in fear today. I live in the light.

As for my family: my mom found AA after she had her left foot amputated due to her alcoholism. My dad died alone in his condo on his kitchen floor. I found him after he had been dead for three days. I know my dad did not die in vain because he showed me how not to do this program. My mom and I both have over six years of continuous sobriety. We both have a sponsor, we both are in service, we both work our Steps, and we both have found our Higher Power.

This program has broken the alcoholic chain in my family tree. God saved me at a very young age and I can honestly say, "I've never had a legal drink in my life."

I know God must have something very special and very important in store for me to have saved me from so much suffering. Don't get me wrong, I've been to jails, institutions, tried to kill myself at eighteen, and put myself through hell. Yet there are so many things I didn't have to do. I reached my bottom when I put the shovel down. My whole life is finally integrated. I do practice these principles in all of my affairs. I'm constantly putting positive information into my brain to record over the "old tapes." I used to say my mind was my worst enemy, but I now realize my mind is one of my most powerful tools.

I can never repay AA for the life I have today, but it's my responsibility to give back freely as God directs me and to remain forever humble, honest, open-minded, and willing to do his will.

Pam H.
Garden Grove, California
June 1995

Wanted

FOURTEEN YEARS OLD and two thousand miles from home, I realized something wasn't right in my life. I had run away from home two months before so that I'd be able to be "on my own." I found myself in Amarillo, Texas. I'd been running with a gang, but now I found myself on the street. I feared the night. I found food in the dumpsters of restaurants until I learned to steal, and stealing became a way of life. It is the way I acquired my booze, my food, my cigarettes, and my clothing. I lived in the fear that some day I'd be caught. Sometimes I got sick to my stomach just thinking about it. It occurred to me that perhaps my life wasn't normal, but the thought would soon pass. This was life as I knew it.

I didn't dream of the day that I'd be a success in a career. Instead, I wanted to go back to the time when drinking was fun, when I could sneak out of the house and return late at night, when drinking didn't bring me pain. I didn't want to be alone anymore. I wanted a friend again.

In the fall of that year, I was placed in an adolescent facility for teenagers with social problems. It was an intense treatment. Most of those with me were convicted criminals. Though I'd also been guilty of crimes, I'd never been caught. The facility was safe and I liked it there. After three and a half months, they released me with the explanation that they were unable to help me. I was diagnosed an alcoholic and AA was strongly suggested.

At the first meeting I attended, I learned of the love that AAs have for each other. I was made to feel welcome. Unlike other organizations, there were no dues or initiation fees. In fact, I was told not to contribute until I'd been there six weeks. AA was different from anything I'd ever heard of. I was wanted.

It has been over seven years since I took a drink. Life hasn't been all smooth sailing, but because of AA, I no longer have to live in fear. I sleep at night. I have a new relationship with my Creator. I have a purpose in life.

Shane L.
Mankato, Minnesota
May 1997

The In Crowd

In the early days of my drinking, I acquired a new lifestyle and it came with a new social circle. This is it, I thought. I've finally found my way to the In Crowd. I belonged. I was cool. This thought came back to me this morning during my meditation, and I realized what being part of the In Crowd brought me. It made me insecure, indecisive, insensible, intolerable, infantile, inebriated, incarcerated a few times, always insane, and at the end, very incomplete.

Mike M.
Sturgeon Falls, Ontario
August 2003

Give Me Enough Rope

I AM PRESENTLY DOING TIME in a maximum security institution for juveniles. I'm not able to attend any meetings, and I feel the need to share some of my experience, strength, and hope in order to stay sober — and help someone else if I can.

I'm a recovering teenage alcoholic. I started drinking on a regular basis at the age of nine or so. My early childhood was filled with the ugliness of alcoholism. My stepfather drank to excess and then he'd beat my mother and me. I told myself that I wouldn't end up like that and I meant it. But somewhere I forgot all that pain; I lost it the first time I got drunk.

My first drunk was a blackout, but I do remember that special feeling the whiskey gave me — the feeling that we alcoholics want to recapture time and time again, regardless of the price we pay or the consequences we endure.

My parents were divorced when I was about ten and I went to live with my mother. It was a long divorce, with them getting together for awhile, then things ending up worse than before. I used anything I could get my hands on in order to escape. I started smoking marijuana out of "necessity" because it was much easier to get hold of. But alcohol remained my drug of choice.

At this time, I started stealing "for the fun of it." I got off on the thrill it gave me. It was another form of escape. I also started getting into trouble with the law and at school.

My mother couldn't control me anymore, so she sent me to live with my stepfather. Again I was in trouble with the law and at school. My drinking increased and my stepfather finally gave up as well. He took me to court, charging me with being unruly, and thus I was made a ward of the court. I was given the choice of going to a foster home or a group home.

I chose what appeared to be the easier of the two. My foster home was with one of the nicest families I've ever met. They were far from rich, but they were full of good old-fashioned love. But alcohol had gotten its hooks in me, and I drank when I could, which wasn't too often. I remember going for bicycle rides and looking for full cans of beer along the road. I found them! During this time, my mother was institutionalized in a mental hospital due to her drinking, and I felt I was to blame because of my actions when I'd lived with her.

After a year with the foster family, I was given the choice of remaining or moving in with my mother. For the sole reason of alcohol, I chose to live with my mother. I thought it would be my dream come true, but in a short time I found it to be more terrible than anything before. One day my mother "went off" and started throwing everything out of the apartment. The police came and she was taken away, tied down to a stretcher. I felt guilty, so I drank excessively from this point on with little care about anything. I believe this is when I crossed that imaginary line of no return.

I went to live with my grandparents, but they weren't equipped to deal with me, so I was sent to live with my aunt and uncle. I got in trouble with the law once again and was expelled from school for good this time. I went back to live with my grandparents, for I had nowhere else to go. During this time, I began eliminating things that I thought were causing me to have problems. Of course, alcohol wasn't one of them. I seemed to think it was others around me, or maybe I was just jinxed when it came to life.

My stay with my grandparents didn't last too long. One night in a blackout, twelve hours after getting my driver's license, I took my grandparents' brand-new customized $16,000 van out for a spin. I was picked up for driving while intoxicated and a long list of other charges. My grandparents gave me a choice: jail for grand theft or a rehabilitation center.

So now I was introduced to the Fellowship of AA. Strange indeed are these folks, I thought to myself. But I could relate. I remember that more than anything else. But ready I was not. My mother was now staying sober with the help of AA, and she told my grandparents to let me run my own course with little interference from them — in other words, give me enough rope to hang myself with. And I did. I kept going on binges every couple of months, each one worse than before. Each time I came closer to death.

On my last drunk, I wrecked my car and killed a close drinking buddy of mine. My world crumbled around me. I saw, at last, the horror of alcoholism. I had a decision to make – either commit suicide or surrender to God and AA.

I will soon be one year sober, one day at a time. I've been locked up for eight months now and am going to be released soon, with God's help. Prison life isn't easy, but it's where I had to get sober. I can't escape myself in here. I have to deal with myself – and the Steps are my keys to freedom.

We can all make it, one day at a time.

Anonymous
Ohio
May 1995

Ten Minutes of Oneness

I'M GRATEFUL I MADE IT TO AA when I was twenty-two years old. I felt at the time that I'd lived forty years of hell. I started drinking when I was thirteen, and I blacked out and got sick right from the start. But the way I felt when the alcohol hit me was worth throwing up for. I remember having ten minutes of complete oneness with the world. I was no longer ugly, stupid, or boring, and I could talk about anything. When I wasn't drinking, I didn't quite fit in this world.

In the beginning, my drinking was mostly on the weekends, but when I got to high school, alcohol became a number-one priority. At night (with a fake ID), I went to bars to have "a few drinks" and would end up with strange people in strange places, coming out of a blackout and not knowing where I was, how I got there, what day it was, where my car was, if I had money left in my wallet. Any values I'd been given by my parents were annihilated when I put alcohol in my system. Drinking produced heart-wrenching shame and remorse when I was dry and the insanity of thinking that another drink would make the pain go away.

I came to a place in my life where I didn't care whether I lived or died. Then what I call miracles started happening in my life. In one of my blackouts, I came to at three o'clock in the morning in my parents' kitchen; two police officers were sitting at the table with me, explaining that I needed to go to the hospital. I had two black eyes, cuts, and bruises – and had no idea what had happened. There was nobody to take me to the hospital, so the officers went through my parents' address book and picked out someone's name and called her and asked her if she could take me. The woman who came was one of our neighbors when I was a child and I hadn't seen her in years. I was checked out by a doctor and was told I'd be okay, but meanwhile, this lady asked me a few questions about my drinking: Did I think I might have a problem with alcohol? I hadn't really thought about it, but I did the next day when I woke up sick, with my head pounding, barely able to get out of bed. When I saw my reflection in the mirror, I was horrified since I couldn't remember what had happened to me. Then suddenly, while I was looking in the mirror, I had my first clear thoughts about drinking: how every time I started drinking, I ended up in trouble, that it was getting worse, and I always ended up drunk.

Through a few other small miracles, I went to my first AA meeting that night. My first reaction was that I was too young to be an alcoholic. I certainly hadn't lost my family, home, husband, etc. – because I'd never had those things in the first place. I hadn't been in jail, and I had no drunk-driving arrests – police officers used to escort me home or to a coffeeshop.

However, at that first meeting, I listened to a woman sharing about how she felt. I couldn't believe that someone felt as I did – different, shy, ashamed, full of guilt and remorse. I was terrified in that meeting, but when it was over I realized I had nothing to lose by checking out AA for a while. I was told to go to ninety meetings in ninety days, and if I didn't like what AA had to offer, I could go back to the misery of my drinking. I was also told not to pick up that first drink because that's the one that would get me drunk. What a profound statement that was. I thought about it for days, trying to figure it out!

I was full of fear in those first few weeks and wouldn't raise my hand to speak. I just wanted to go from feeling terrible to feeling bad — a step up at the time. It was suggested I get a sponsor and I thank God I did; I was afraid of the woman I asked, yet at the same time I liked her because she had a sparkle in her eyes. (She still does!) I was able to talk to her and ask questions. Talking to her helped me start sharing myself in meetings.

I came to accept that I was an alcoholic when I was sober about six months. At the time there weren't many people around who were my age, but fortunately I was taken under the wings of gracious AA members and spoiled with tough love. It's ten years later and I'm still sober. I'm very active in AA. I don't think I could ever give back what has been given to me but I try to thank God and AA for this gift in one way or another every day.

My drinking experience also involved the use of other chemicals, but I feel that's unnecessary to share at AA meetings. When I brought up this "controversy" with my sponsor, she told me to read the Traditions and come to my own conclusion about what was right for me. I love the Fellowship of Alcoholics Anonymous and I think the more I change, the more I hope the Traditions and principles of AA don't change. I believe it's my responsibility to support the Traditions and live the principles. I'm not here to change Alcoholics Anonymous; Alcoholics Anonymous is here to change me. Thank God.

D. W.
San Mateo, California
December 1995

Rarely Have We Seen a Person Fail . . .

ITOOK MY FIRST REAL DRINK, aside from sips of beer from family members, the summer after eighth grade. I was thirteen years old and baby-sitting with my cousin. She mixed some vodka and orange juice and without even thinking, I began to drink. It was one of those things, like smoking, that I swore I'd never do because I saw how it made my alcoholic family members act and I didn't want to be like them. The compulsion began immediately. Suddenly, I was beautiful and smart and funny, and everyone loved me. We continued to drink until we ran out of orange juice. One of us got the bright idea to mix the rest of the vodka with fudge ripple ice cream. The rest of the night is pretty blurry: it was my first time getting drunk and I experienced my first blackout. I later thought that this was normal, since I experienced them nearly every time I drank. All I know for sure is that right away I felt like I couldn't get enough. I got sick, and the parents came home to me throwing up in their cast-iron skillet on their kitchen table. My cousin told them I had gotten food poisoning, even though I can only imagine how I smelled.

The next morning I woke up sicker than I had ever been before. I had several earrings in my ear that I didn't have the previous day, and there was some kind of fluid all over my bed. I'm still not sure what it was or where it came from. I was scared and I was sick, but I also felt somehow whole. It was like I had finally found something I'd been looking for all my life. The suicide attempts, the running away, the faking illnesses — none of these had worked for me and I'd been trying them for as long as I could remember. But the alcohol, that was different. I had finally found something that made me feel like I was someone else. Someone better. Not me.

From that point on, I drank and got drunk whenever I could. I stole alcohol from my parents and brought it over to my friends' houses. I stole it from my friends' parents and anywhere else I could find it. My friends got tired of the new me pretty quickly, and it's not hard to understand why. Every time I drank, I got sick and out of control. I was normally a very quiet and shy person, but when I drank I became loud and obnoxious. Eventually, I always ended up in a bathroom somewhere, passed out with my head in the toilet. My teenage years were proving to be very glamorous!

It wasn't long after I started drinking that I turned to drugs. I used drugs like I drank; whatever I could get, whenever I could get it, as much as

I could. I soon began selling drugs to support my addiction. Alcohol was a constant by now and I used it for maintenance. Drugs brought me over the edge when I felt I needed it.

Pretty soon, it all stopped working for me. That feeling of being beautiful and funny and loved was gone. Now I not only felt different and lost when I was not drinking, but the lostness seemed to be magnified when I was under the influence of something. I tried using more and more to get that magical feeling back, but nothing was working anymore. I remember thinking that I knew I had a problem because my life was like an After-School Special about alcoholics and drug addicts.

I had what I guess I would call the usual problems of a teenage alcoholic: I started to get in trouble with the police for things like shoplifting, underage consumption, and trespassing. I drank my way through several sets of friends, always finding new people to hang out with when the old ones got tired of my behavior. I was not fun to be around. I set limits for myself every night on how much I would drink and I always went over. My friends would tell me what I had done or said the next day.

I knew I had a problem and that I couldn't stop drinking. I'd seen some family members with the same problem. No one had ever said anything about a way to quit, so at seventeen I thought that I was destined to live my life as a drunk. It didn't much matter to me at this point. I didn't think I would live that long anyway. I was so depressed that I figured I'd either kill myself in a short time or I'd end up dying in some accident while I was in a blackout. That's when God stepped in.

It was my senior year and I'd been selling LSD around school. The Friday night that started off my winter break, I was planning on going to a party. I stopped by my parents' house to get the address, and when I walked in they had this look on their faces like someone had just died. My little brother was sitting in the living room crying. He wouldn't look at me or talk to me. My parents brought me into the kitchen and told me that a detective had been there looking for me. They asked if I had any idea what he could have wanted with me. Of course, I told them I didn't. They knew about most of the trouble I had already gotten into, but they really wanted to believe that I was a good person and I played that role in front of them as best as I could.

They told me that the detective hadn't told them what he was there for, even though I found out later that he had. They brought me into the police station to talk to him. He sat us down and explained to me that a girl I had sold LSD to a few months before had freaked out and gone to the hospital. She'd told the police that I had been the one to sell it to her. I'd been under surveillance for two months. I had been followed everywhere I went and had a tap on my phone. They said they had talked to some of my friends and schoolmates, and they knew that I was the one who had sold LSD to this girl as well as many other people. If anyone decided to press charges, I would be charged with attempted murder.

I remember thinking, "How am I going to get out of this one?" I tried to put a look of disbelief on my face, like I was so innocent I couldn't believe they were accusing me. It didn't work. My parents took me home that night and gave me the lecture on how much, once again, I had disappointed them. They searched my room for paraphernalia, then left me alone. I was busted. I felt like my whole world was crumbling down. I knew that I was alone.

I decided to stay clean and sober, because I knew I was going to have to go to court. I had a real incentive this time, and I was actually able to do it, but not without a price. The first week I was clean I lay in bed under the covers and shook. I screamed at anyone who came into my room and at people who weren't there. The paranoia and fear I felt was overwhelming. I thought I was going to die.

I began to slowly get better, physically anyway. By the time I went back to school, I wasn't getting sick anymore. The girl who had turned me in ended up being in two of my classes. I hated her more than anything. I thought she was responsible for my pain. I always had to have someone or something else to blame for the way I was feeling, and she was perfect this time.

17

Somehow, one day in gym class the girl and I ended up running laps next to each other. She had tried to talk to me before, but I'd always ignored her and given her dirty looks. For some reason, that day I heard the words "What's up?" come out of my mouth, and we started talking. I know today that God was completely responsible for this one. A week later she called me up to ask if I wanted to go to a meeting. I had no idea what she was talking about and she explained to me that she had been able to stay sober by going to AA meetings and working the Twelve Steps. I told her thanks, but no thanks. I was doing just fine on my own.

But that phone call really made me start thinking. Was I doing fine on my own? What about my obsession to go back to drinking and using drugs? The threat of court wasn't enough anymore. I wanted to drink and I didn't care what the consequences were. I decided to try one of these meetings with her the following week.

I remember very little about my first meeting. They probably had a First Step meeting for me, but all I know for certain is that I cried the whole time. It didn't matter that everyone else there was much older than me. I finally felt that I had found a place where I belonged.

I drank one more time after this meeting. I told my friends not to tell anyone because I was afraid the people at the meeting would find out. I was ashamed and I knew I was acting like an alcoholic — just like the people at the meeting had described. I didn't decide then that would be my last time drinking, but from that day to this I have not had to pick up another drink. I know I owe that to AA.

I slowly started going to meetings and slowly started taking the suggestions and working the Steps. I was hardheaded and wanted to do things my way, so it took a long time for me to start feeling really better. Something told me that things were going to be okay if I kept going to meetings and didn't drink. It was very hard and very painful, but one day at a time I was able to keep coming back until the miracle happened.

When I was about two years sober, I was sitting in a First Step meeting, telling my story, when suddenly I came to believe that getting busted was the best thing that ever happened to me. If it hadn't been for that, I would never have found the program that I so desperately needed. I had been so resentful over that situation, but now I could be grateful for it. I believe that was my first miracle, and I've experienced many since then.

I am now twenty-four years old, and I just celebrated my seven-year anniversary in AA. The only way it's worked for me is to do what others have done in the past: don't drink, go to meetings, get a sponsor, and read the Big Book. It can be a very painful process, especially in the beginning and even now, but I've been given the tools to get through the pain and get to the gratitude. I've been able to see some of the Promises come true in my life, and I truly believe that is a miracle. I was able to get through the rest of high school and college sober. I have a job that I love today and people in my life whom I love. Everything I have I owe to AA. Most important, AA has given me a relationship with God. This has allowed me not only to stay sober one day at a time, but to live a full and meaningful life.

This is an incredible Fellowship and I'm very grateful to be a part of it, although I don't always feel this way. Sometimes I feel very sorry for myself, because I'm young and I'm an alcoholic and I'm never going to be able to drink again. When I start to think like this, I remember that this is a one-day-at-a-time program and that God has a plan for me. I was brought to this Fellowship at exactly the right time. I drank as much as I needed to get here and felt as much pain as I needed to. I've already been fortunate enough to see how my experience as a young person in AA can benefit others. I attend an AA meeting at a treatment center for adolescent girls. So many of these girls tell me that they can relate to me and that maybe AA can help them, too. I don't know how many of them stay sober once they get out of treatment, but that really doesn't matter. They help to keep me sober one day at a time, because they help me remember where I was and why I got here when I did.

Thankfully, there isn't a set amount that we have to drink or certain things that we have to lose for us to become members of this Fellowship. I always remember that "the only requirement for membership is a desire to stop drinking." I know I have this desire, so I will keep coming back.

Jennifer B.
Libertyville, Illinois
July 1999

My Sneakers Never Looked As Good As Yours

ALTHOUGH I ONLY DRANK FOR FIVE YEARS, I *am* an alcoholic. I was born with this disease and I will die with this disease. Without AA, I would be dead. I am so grateful for this program. It has given me eleven years of sobriety this month. Everything I am is a direct result of God and AA.

When I speak, I talk about my childhood a little, not because I blame anything that happened for my alcoholism. I talk about it because I believe I was born with this disease. Whether I came from a mansion or a cardboard box, I would still be an alcoholic.

As a child I always felt different. I like to say I had a God hole. I was filled with fear. I never felt like I measured up. I always just fell short. I judged my insides by everyone's outsides. They all looked so happy. I wanted to feel the way they looked. I just didn't know how to get there.

I come from a loving home. Alcohol was always present, but I wouldn't consider it an alcoholic home. I was adopted at age three but I was never made to feel different. Yet I was always filled with fear. And that God hole was always there.

The best way I can describe the way I felt is with my sneaker story. When I was a kid, sneakers were a big thing. If you had a cool pair of sneakers, then you were cool. So I would see a cool pair of sneakers on someone and I would go out and get the same pair as they had. But for some reason my sneakers didn't look as good on me as they did on other people. I was in constant turmoil. If I could have unzipped my skin and crawled out, I would have. I was always searching for a way to feel okay, something that would take the fear away.

I had my first drink at age eleven. I had seen drinking as a kid. I noticed before people started drinking they were quiet. But after a few drinks, they seemed to be happy. I wanted what they had. So a friend and I raided his mother's liquor cabinet one night. I had a little bit of everything. And then it happened! For the first time in my life, I felt okay. The fear was gone. And my sneakers were as good as everybody else's, and if they weren't, it didn't matter. I could talk to people, I was as good as, and I measured up to. I knew then that I was going to drink whenever I could.

The "Twelve and Twelve" says that "alcohol the rapacious creditor, bleeds us of all self-sufficiency and will to resist its demands." "Rapacious" means "feeds on living prey." When I look back, I realize that alcohol robbed me blind. It stole family, opportunities, and finally my desire to live. At the end, I prayed for death.

I became a violent alcoholic. I got in a lot of trouble with the police. At the age of fourteen, I got my first unlicensed DWI. Six months after that I got my second DWI. I got into fights and got locked up in a ten-by-ten holding cell several times. Each time I got locked up, I'd say to myself, "How could this have happened again? This time it was going to be different." It never was any different. But I believed alcohol took away the fear. I wasn't prepared to give that up.

The minute I picked up the first drink I no longer had control of how much I would have or what I was going to do. I sat downstairs with my bottle of whiskey like a mad scientist, trying to figure out the right mix so that I could drink normally.

I did what alcohol told me. What choice did I have?

I came around AA for about a year before I got sober. From my first meeting I knew I belonged. I just thought I was too young. People would tell me when I came back in, "You never have to feel this way again." In December 1987, through the grace of God and AA, I finally believed that

21

in my heart. This program gave me hope even when I didn't want it. AA people made me feel okay. God filled the God hole. Everything I looked for in a bottle I found in AA.

My life is beautiful today. I stay close to AA. I try to help another alcoholic. I am active in my home group. I got my driver's license, I turned twenty-one, got married, had a son, and I did it all sober. To all the young people out there who are unsure, I want to say, "Keep coming back, no matter what." Enjoy the gift of sobriety and try to pass it on.

I would like to close with a line from a prayer I read: "I asked God for all things that I may enjoy life. I was given life that I might enjoy all things."

John L.
Howell, New Jersey
September 1999

Far from Innocent

WHEN I ENTERED ALCOHOLICS ANONYMOUS, I was twenty-one years old. Notice that I did not say "only twenty-one," but "twenty-one." I have never heard people say they came in when they were "only forty-eight," so why should I be any different? Being in AA for over a year now, I have noticed that people respond differently to young AA members than they do to older members of the Fellowship. At meetings, people will say, "It's so nice to see you young people here tonight!" To this day, I have not heard that said about the older members or the old-timers. Why not? It's good to see them too, right? It's nice to see any alcoholic, of any age, on any given night.

Older members tell me how lucky I am that I didn't have to go through what they did. How do they know what I went through? The circumstances and duration of time might be different, but the emotional hell is the same or similar. The Big Book tells me that one does not have to drink long to be gravely affected, as does my own life experience. Eight years of drinking caused me to give away everything I had, physically and emotionally. My family would no longer speak with me, and by my own doing, I was forced to live on the street. Having no social or employable skills, I stole and panhandled in order to survive. More importantly, though, I lost my dignity, self-respect, and dreams of ever having a fulfilling life. Did I lose enough, or should I have lost more? The only thing I didn't lose by coming in so young is years of time. If I was so lucky to be here, why didn't I win the lottery? Luck did not get me here, God did.

Why do people assume that a person is brand-new if he or she is young? A friend of mine, eighteen years old, has over three years of sobriety, yet people constantly treat him as if he is new. In the beginning, the phrase "Keep coming back" was encouraging. Today, it is insulting. If someone says that to me, it is because they have stereotyped me. Maybe people feel that we are not serious about sobriety, but that is a misconception. I take sobriety seriously, but try not to do that with life.

Young people are not "kids"; they are young adults. Many of us come from broken homes and shattered lives and have not been "kids" for many years. Do not judge us by our innocent appearance, for many of us are far from innocent. Do not condescend to us, because we are intelligent and you damage your attempt to be useful. Instead, love us as you would any other member in the family of Alcoholics Anonymous. What we lack in wisdom, we make up in enthusiasm and spirit. If I said I killed someone because I got behind the wheel intoxicated, would you take me seriously then? How old do you have to be to destroy someone else's life?

Young and old and everything in-between, we are all in this together. Without the older generation, there would have been no one to carry the message to me. Saying thank-you would not be enough, but my appreciation can be shown by carrying the message to the next generation. We are definitely people who normally would not mix, but we are definitely not normal people. Despite our many differences, the harmony in which we get along and coexist is truly amazing.

Young alcoholics are real alcoholics and should not be treated with indifference, but with compassion and understanding. We should not be treated as special cases or with sugar-coated sobriety. Do not pamper us or pinch our cheeks, because we are the same as you. Our suffering and sickness were no different than yours, so why should our recovery be?

Justin W.
St. Petersburg, Florida
March 2003

Fun to Spare

IN THE OCTOBER 1986 GRAPEVINE, a report on the 27th International Conference of Young People in AA contained an apocryphal story about an AA old-timer who happened to be a Texas Ranger. The Ranger, it was told, "sat by himself in the back of the AA meeting room behind a pair of dark sunglasses, with his silver spurs propped up on the table in front of him, and his hundred-dollar cowboy hat tipped back onto his sunburned forehead.

"Well, one day a young fellow showed up at the meeting in pretty bad shape. He was cut and bleeding, and what clothes he had left reeked of alcohol. Some of the older members of the group quickly got to their feet and ushered the ragged newcomer to the front of the room where they began to tell him what AA was all about. After a pretty good earful, the newcomer took a skeptical look around him.

"'Maybe I'm too young for all this,' he said. 'You mean I have to stay away from the first drink, come to these meetings, and never have any more fun?'

"From the back of the room the Texas Ranger's spurs clanked to the floor like a gunshot. He got up from his seat and a path cleared in front of him as he sidled up to the newcomer. The Ranger bent down, lifted up his sunglasses, and looked straight into the newcomer's bloodshot eyes. "'Son,' he asked, 'just how much damned fun can you *stand*?'"

The Foundation

"How will I know if I've really hit my bottom?" I asked at my home group. "When you stop digging," they told me. The bottom is only the bottom until we find AA. The day we begin working the Steps, the bottom becomes the foundation. By taking action and following the program, we begin to build our lives again.

Bob G.
Chelsea, Michigan
November 2002

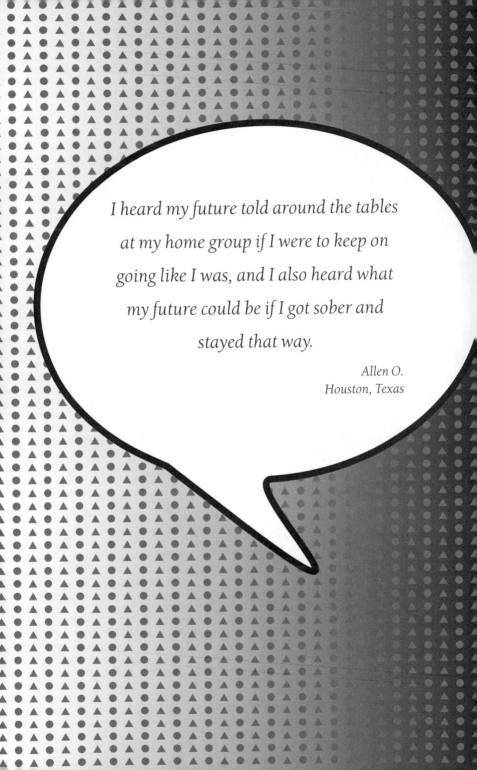

I heard my future told around the tables at my home group if I were to keep on going like I was, and I also heard what my future could be if I got sober and stayed that way.

Allen O.
Houston, Texas

Section Two: **WELCOME — YOU ARE NOT ALONE**

Above All, an Alcoholic

SCARED OUT OF MY WITS, sick, shaking, confused, lonely, I drove past that AA hall again and again, waiting until the last possible moment before I had to open that door. I had been at this point before and always had some "good" reason for backing out. This time, there were no reasons. All that was left at the ripe old age of twenty-five were the ruins of a young family.

But what was going to happen when I walked through that door? What were those people going to ask me? How could I tell them that I might have a drinking problem, that I didn't know what was happening in my life anymore, that I had squandered thousands of dollars, that I hurt people and hated myself, that I was married and had a little girl, and that I was gay? Oh God, they wouldn't understand. They'd look at me with utter disgust, incredulity, and righteous judgment in their eyes.

Pain is a great motivator. I got out of the car, took a few breaths, held my head up, and walked toward that door. "If it's too awful," I said to myself, "I can leave." I had become quite accustomed to rejection. "There are not a whole lot of people who could understand," I told myself. "So what's one more time? I don't know where else to go."

I opened the door and walked into the warmth, the laughter, the acceptance, and the love that is AA. No one asked me who I was or what I wanted; no one asked me how much money I had or what I did for a living; no one asked me where I did my drinking or what my sexual preferences were. The smiling man who greeted me told me that if I thought I had a drinking problem, I was in the right place. "Don't compare your story to the one you'll hear tonight," he suggested. "Try to relate to what he says, to what alcohol did to him as a human being."

Well, my Higher Power was apparently working overtime that night, because I did relate to the speaker. When he was finished, I knew I was an alcoholic, not a lunatic, not an evil, immoral wretch, but a sick person suffering from a disease of body, mind, and spirit, and if I wanted to get well, AA could help. And it has.

The process of getting and staying sober has been far from easy. Years' worth of guilt, self-hatred, resentment, and fear don't go away overnight. It takes a lot of work, a lot of prayer. Above all, it requires physical sobriety. But believe me, it does get better.

The first year I was sober, nearly all my energy went into AA: meetings, meetings, meetings; getting as active as I could; reading and studying the Big Book and *Twelve Steps and Twelve Traditions*; visiting institutions and rehab centers; talking with new people about the program; going along on Twelfth Step calls and to AA conferences and social gatherings; and slowly, ever so slowly opening up to these people, whom I found I could trust.

Time passed quickly, and I discovered one day (with the help of an old-timer) that I, too, had learned how to stay sober. He told me that I looked healthy, had a genuine smile now, and had that "AA look" in my eyes. I was made aware that my ballooned ego was being replaced with self-respect, that resentment and hatred were being replaced with tolerance and understanding, that fear was being replaced with trust, and that loneliness and self-pity were being replaced with gratitude and love – all because I was working the program to the best of my ability and wasn't drinking.

I kept coming back as I was told, for there was – and still is – much work to do. When the time arrived for me to deal with what I thought was the most hideous aspect of my character, I was able to. With the help of a Higher Power and the people in AA, I made it and am making it, sometimes tearfully but more often joyfully. When I entered AA, two and one-half years ago, there were no gay groups in our area. I didn't know where to turn. Slowly, as I became ready, God put people in my life – some gay, some not, some new people, some old-timers. We have stayed sober and grown together. By applying the principles and program of AA, I have gained my freedom – freedom to be myself, to like myself as I am, to become whatever it is that my Higher Power has planned for me, one day at a time – freedom to live the type of life I'm most comfortable with, to love, and to laugh.

29

If there is one slogan in the program that is more important than another to me, it is "First Things First." Above all else, I must remember that I am an alcoholic, that I must remain willing to go to any length to maintain my sobriety, or I will die. Gay or straight, black or white, Jew or Christian, rich or poor, it won't make a bit of difference if I choose to drink. For with me, as with every alcoholic, to drink is to die.

J. B.
Toledo, Ohio
September 1982

Just Visiting?

I WAS SIX YEARS OLD when I had my first drink. It was vodka. I had found heaven. For the next seven years I periodically snuck drinks from my parent's liquor cabinet.

By the time I was thirteen, I had found friends who liked to do the same. It started out just on the weekends, two or three times a month. It was always with the same goal in mind – getting as drunk as possible.

In seventh grade something changed. My friends began to say things like, "Slow down" or "You drink too much. Maybe you should quit." My answer to this was to find new friends.

By the time I was in ninth grade, my drinking career had taken off. I found a group of "friends" who could obtain alcohol and sell drugs. I began ingesting other chemicals. I no longer cared about others. I was losing control of my life. Blackouts were frequent, and unfortunately so was waking up in strange places next to people I didn't recognize, wondering what had happened.

A friend of mine began attending AA meetings because his mother thought he had a problem. He asked me if I wanted to go. I saw it as a way to get out of the house so I went. I'd never even heard of Alcoholics

Anonymous and didn't know what to expect.

I walked up those long steps and came to a large, smoky room that I would later call home. I was the youngest person in the room. Everyone seemed at least twice my age. I began rationalizing why I didn't belong. Then I figured out that it didn't matter anyway because I had no desire to quit and was only there for my friend. The meeting started. The chairperson asked if anyone was there for their first meeting. I knew everyone was looking at me so I raised my hand. The chairperson said, "Are you here for yourself or to support someone else?" I said, "Oh no, I'm here for him," pointing at my friend. A few people smiled. It didn't occur to me then that they were smiling because they'd been in my shoes. I was in denial because I hadn't suffered enough. I don't remember the rest of that meeting or the next five I attended. I stopped going because I had no desire to quit yet.

I was once told that we hit bottom when we put down the shovel and quit digging. I didn't put down the shovel for another year. Within that year I lost the trust of my family, and all my friends deserted me (with good reason). I put myself in a bad situation one night and was raped because I was so drunk I couldn't move or call for help. By this time stealing and lying had become a way of life. I could no longer look in the mirror at my reflection because it made me sick. I stopped eating and bathing for days at a time. I tried to commit suicide several times but I guess my Higher Power had something else in mind. I was no longer living, just existing. I dreaded waking up in the morning because it meant I was still alive. The alcohol wasn't working anymore.

That friend who had taken me to my first AA meeting had put together thirty days. He took me to a meeting and a guy came up to me after the meeting and asked if I wanted to talk. I thought to myself, "Oh great, this guy just wants to hit on me." Then something happened. All the walls I had built came crumbling down. I ended up telling him where the previous year had taken me. He gave me a hug and I felt AA start to work for me. That was November 17, 1990. I haven't had to pick up a drink since then.

I'm twenty-three years old now. Sobriety has been far from easy. I made it hard on myself and didn't do what was suggested to me. I finally got so miserable in my second year that I either had to change or get drunk again. I wasn't afraid of dying; I was afraid of living another twenty or thirty years in that despair and hopelessness.

I got a sponsor and really began working the Steps. I read the literature and threw myself into service work. I chaired meetings and became secretary of my home group. I now sponsor people as well.

I know what real friendship is today. I know how to love today. Life hasn't always been easy, but I wouldn't trade my worst day sober for my best day drunk.

Denise T.
Bremerton, Washington
September 1998

Around the Tables

My name is Allen and I am an alcoholic. I came into AA when I was fifteen years old. At first I couldn't understand anything about the Steps, Traditions, or Big Book except the phrase I heard at meetings: "Keep coming back, it works."

After going back out twice at the start of the recovery process, today I have over seven years, one day at a time. I heard my future told around the tables at my home group if I were to keep on going like I was, and I also heard what my future could be if I got sober and stayed that way.

Now I know what they mean when I hear, "You have to give it away in order to keep it."

Allen O.
Houston, Texas
October 1994

Anything to Be Cool

I BEGAN DRINKING and taking drugs when I was fourteen years old. It was the year 1994 and the rebellious songs of Green Day and Offspring surrounded the world of the fourteen-year-old. We were a generation inspired by the skater crowd, the nineties' version of the sixties' greasers and the eighties' punk rockers. To be in the cool crowd, you had to wear clothes eight sizes too big, walk cool, smoke cigarettes and pot, and drink beer. In those days, I would have jumped off a 100-foot cliff if it meant I could be considered cool. Drinking a petty beer or smoking a little joint was an insignificant hurdle for me on my road to social acceptance. After all, I was invincible and the worse the action, the more attention I would receive. I attended the Drug Abuse Resistance Education (D.A.R.E.) classes and sat through countless drug-prevention speeches, but those did not apply to such a cool rebel without a cause.

Just eight years later, I found myself unable to complete the simplest of tasks without an anxiety attack or to stick with a job for more than two months before getting fired for my habitual tardiness. Today, with the help of the program of Alcoholics Anonymous, my life consists of re-learning how to complete a full day without acting on my impulses. I am bombarded with feelings of pain and strife that I cannot even begin to explain. I have watched this disease take the life of my aunt and destroy the lives of my mother, grandparents, uncles, and cousins. To this day, I am amazed that you can watch a loved one die a slow and painful death from alcoholism, only to go home at night and consume the same death potion yourself. Most of all, I am saddened by the ignorance and denial in our society.

I believe that it is only through my willingness to completely turn my life over to AA that I have the chance of recovering a life of any value. This is a program that has not only saved millions of lives, but has single-handedly reshaped and almost eliminated the absolute helplessness that this willing-to-recover alcoholic used to experience. This is a program that, through

33

faith and action, slowly allows an alcoholic to recover from spiritual, physical, mental, and financial bankruptcy.

Alcoholics Anonymous, I believe, is built on the foundation that no matter what one's religion, race, creed, gender, or degree of hopelessness, its members will do anything in their power to help. Therefore, I can walk into a meeting anywhere in the country and find a room full of the broke and the rich, the powerful and the powerless, the famous and the ordinary citizen. Anonymity makes us all equal and everyone feel welcome. This anonymity is what gave me the courage to walk through those doors. It's what gives me the strength to keep coming back.

Elliot H.
Manhattan, Montana
June 2004

Angels on the Internet

WHEN I STARTED DRINKING at the age of sixteen, I drank to get drunk, even though I wasn't even sure what "drunk" was. Every time I did drink, trouble inevitably followed. After each night of drinking, I always ended up feeling guilty and ashamed, not to mention sick and hungover.

Those feelings of guilt and remorse eventually came to a head one night when I was staying with my extended family. There was no booze in the house, and I was trying to fall asleep. Nor was there TV to drown out the thoughts that ran through my head. I started to wonder what had happened to myself – to my life. I was twenty-four years old and realized that the dreams I had as a child somehow had faded away. My ambition had vanished, and my future seemed dismal. That was the night, with my Higher Power's help, that I made the connection between the emptiness I was feeling and my abuse of alcohol. From that point on, I thought it was all up to me. I thought it was about willpower, and I made a conscious decision not to drink.

I managed to dry out for a while – several months even. However, I knew there was something missing, something I couldn't quite put my finger on. I didn't know how much longer I could manage, even though I wanted so badly not to have to drink again. I was at a crossroad, but I had no idea where it would lead.

The turning point came about in a way I like to call "a sign of the times." My family had just bought a computer, and we were all having fun with it. One night, my uncle (who had seventeen years of sobriety at that time) went into a chat room where the topic was alcoholism. I was sitting right next to him, intrigued with how they were talking about what they did to stay sober. A couple of nights after that, when everyone in the house was asleep, I went back to the same chat room and confided to these people (strangers!) that I was trying not to drink, but didn't know how much longer I could hold out. They started asking me questions like, "Do you have a sponsor?" and "How many meetings do you go to?" When I answered, "Oh, I'm not in AA or anything like that," they asked me, simply, "Why not?" They told me flat out that if I thought I had any kind of problem with alcohol, I owed it to myself to go to a meeting. Or two. Or three.

By the time I finished talking with these angels on the Internet (about ten hours later!), they had convinced me to try a meeting. A thrill went through me when I found the local hotline number in the phone book. An even bigger thrill went through me when I went to a meeting and heard the chairperson talk about the things I had been going through. And all this happened a mere twelve hours after, helpless and hopeless, I had logged on to the Internet and seen that there was hope.

Kathy C.S.
Ukiah, California
February 2001

AA Campus

M E? Start a new meeting? "Don't we have enough meetings around here?" I said to my sponsor. "Why do we need another one?"

My protests fell on deaf ears, and off we went to start the process of forming a new meeting. I was eighteen months sober and feeling very comfortable with my meeting schedule and my AA friends. Four or five evening meetings and two lunchtime meetings a week gave me all the AA I wanted.

My sponsor thought otherwise. He saw a need for a Friday night meeting at one of the local universities. The fall semester was just starting and it was the perfect time to start a new meeting. I didn't agree with him. Friday night was the night my home group met. Every Friday night four AA meetings, two Al-Anon meetings, and an Alateen meeting were held in the same building. The group had been in existence for many years before I got there, but I felt that I was an important (read: irreplaceable) part of it. I had dozens of friends there and besides, it was convenient for my wife and children to attend their meetings with me.

We had a meeting for beginners, a Step and Traditions meeting, a closed discussion, and a young people's meeting. We had everything and besides, I didn't even know how to start a new meeting. "Call the university administration office and find out what we have to do" were my instructions.

"What if they don't want to have an AA meeting on their campus? What if someone recognizes me? What will I say? What will I do?" I whined some more.

"Try to act like a sober alcoholic," was his sarcastic reply. "And be sure to tell them that we pay our own way."

A telephone call to the main university number got me a very confused operator who connected me with the medical clinic. The person I spoke with suggested I call the community relations department. The young lady in the community relations department seemed to have more on the ball than my first two contacts. Perhaps it had something to do with my being able to make more sense with her than with the other two. By the time I got through to her, I had pretty much gotten over my paranoia that they would find out who I was, and my name, photo, and AA affiliation would be published in the next edition of the campus newspaper.

The next morning I casually (trying not to look like an alcoholic) strolled into the administration office and announced to the receptionist that I had an appointment with Miss M. "Mr. O. (she stated my full name) from AA is here to see you," she announced into the telephone. I knew that the crowds (two students) waiting in the reception room had heard her and were now pointing at me. I felt dozens of eyes boring into my back as I hurried down the hall looking for Miss M.'s office. My serenity and my anonymity were destroyed.

I met with a pleasant lady who was not only very receptive to our idea but actually jumped at the chance to help us and promised the full support of the university. She readily agreed to everything I requested. Yes, we could have the meeting on Friday night. In fact, she thought that was perfect since more students drank on Friday nights than during the week. I wasn't sure whether we would be a deterrent to that practice, but since she was giving, I was listening.

Yes, they had a room available. The meetings could be held in the student union building. If we insisted (we did), there would be a very nominal flat charge for the use of a room and we could work out a storage arrangement for a coffeepot, literature, and supplies with the janitor.

"Great," I said. "May I see the room?"

The large student union building had a two-story-high main hall with floor-to-ceiling glass-fronted meeting rooms encircling it on the ground floor. The central hall had several TVs surrounded by chairs and sofas. A rathskeller was in full operation downstairs on Friday and Saturday nights. Various campus organizations rented the room for parties, most of which served beer. "Do I really want to do this? This will be like meeting in an aquarium," I thought. Fearing my sponsor's wrath, I pressed on. We were given a standing Friday night reservation for one of the rooms.

Signs were posted on bulletin boards and a notice was placed in the campus newspaper. On Friday night my sponsor, three more of his pigeons, and I made a pot of coffee, set out some literature donated by other groups, taped an "AA Meeting" sign on the door, and at 8:30 P.M. we opened our new AA meeting with the Serenity Prayer. No one pointed at us or made faces through the window. We did receive some stares through those glass walls as we held hands and recited the Lord's Prayer at the close of the meeting, but we came back the next Friday.

No students showed up that night or for the next six or seven weeks. We received support from the other groups in the area and our little open discussion meeting usually had eight or ten AAs in attendance. Sponsors brought their pigeons and the word got around. We got our first student after about two months. He was not new to AA, but he stayed and became a regular. Several other students came to a few meetings and then disappeared. Most of them had been steered to the meeting by the university clinic. Even though they didn't stay, they learned enough to know that AA was there when they wanted it.

I celebrated my second anniversary at that little meeting. We had a small cake and several of my friends attended. It was a special anniversary and one I will always remember. A young woman walked into our meeting that night. She was a student and wanted help. She stayed. A year later she celebrated her first anniversary with us. That was nineteen years ago. We still share our anniversary date.

It was a difficult meeting to keep going. We couldn't maintain any continuity. The student union was closed during the Thanksgiving and Christmas holidays and during the summer. The meeting lasted another year or so, but we never attracted any more students who stayed with us.

That campus meeting was the first of many new meetings that I have helped to start over the years. The campus meeting is physically gone now, but its spirit is still working. The walk-ins were given the opportunity to be exposed to AA. Maybe some of them are sober today. Many of the people who maintained their sobriety because that meeting was there are still sober. They, in turn, are still carrying the message to other alcoholics.

Bill O.
Henrico, North Carolina
September 2001

How to Give a Lead

I WAS ENCOURAGED to give the lead at my home group. It is a rite of passage, I was told, a part of the Twelfth Step. I said I would think about it.

I am a lousy speaker. Sometimes I forget to breathe, and in the middle of a sentence, I have to gulp for air or turn blue. Sometimes saliva runs down the corners of my mouth like the spittle on an old man.

No, no way. But it happened anyway. I am not good at thinking on my feet; giving an ad-lib speech is beyond my limits and wishes. My lead has to be perfect – one that rocks the rafters and leaves the listeners awestruck. I would have to outline my lead, write it down, transfer it to index cards, memorize and practice, know when to throw in a little humor to lighten my deep thoughts, all the time building hurdles that I couldn't jump even if I were bourbon-reinforced.

I was embarrassed at my story. It was dull. In the first Steps of recovery, as I took personal and moral inventory and made amends, even I was bored. I was just a drunk who drank too much and did not care. I knew that drinking was a slow death, but I was in no hurry.

I didn't start drinking at the age of ten, was never beaten or molested, never jailed, never stole a police car and drove 110 miles an hour down the expressway the wrong way, never lost a wife or children, never had my parents change the locks on the door. I'd done nothing no one hadn't heard before. Somebody's boring and I think it's me.

One evening the guest lead speaker couldn't make the meeting. The chair looked around the room, asking if there was anyone who had never given a lead. No matter how small I shrank in my chair and stared at the ceiling, I couldn't hide.

Okay. Since God got me to AA, certainly he wouldn't let me down now. He didn't.

I stumbled, I rambled, I hemmed and hawed. I said, "Oh, I forgot to tell the part about . . ." and wiped the spit from my mouth.

Then God came through. I wasn't giving a speech to a crowd. I was talking to friends in my living room. They were listening to me! They were interested and they cared. I was so excited at being useful that I forgot to be frightened. At the end, there was applause. A veteran member came to me and said, "I've never heard a lead given just that way."

I took it as a compliment.

Ron B.
Harrison, Ohio
July 2005

Rescued

I love the community of recovering people. Our stories are authentic, heartbreaking, miraculous, and very funny. We are dancing on the graves that nearly pulled us under, and we know that our rescue from our other lives is a gift.

Liz O.
Oakland, California
April 2006

What Have I Got to Lose?

D URING THIS MORNING'S QUIET TIME, I started wondering if I needed to go to last night's meeting. I'm almost thirteen years sober, have some serenity in my life, am active in district and area service work, have a wonderful family and a great job. I know with certainty that I owe all of this to AA.

My wife made a promise to me early in sobriety, when I was doing what my sponsor said and going to a meeting every day, that she saw the change in me and would never ask me to stay home from a meeting. But this morning, I started wondering: Did I need to go to last night's meeting? If I had not gone to that meeting what would have happened? Would I have drunk? Probably not. Would I have lost some degree of serenity? Probably not. Would I have quit doing service work? Probably not. Would I have lost my family or my job? Again, probably not. Then what would have happened if I had missed last night's meeting? I would have missed Dianne, three weeks out of jail and newly sober, celebrating her fortieth "belly button" birthday with a call from her mother. I would have missed Wade and Les, driving 170 miles to the meeting because they hadn't been there for a while. I would have missed Jim talk about relapsing after twenty-eight years when he'd stopped going to meetings. I would have missed Joe realize the promise of losing the fear of economic insecurity. I would have missed Bill share how he was able to hand-make gifts for his grandchildren, something that they will always have to remember him by. I would have missed John share forty-five years of sobriety, one day at a time.

I have learned that I have only today. I can't live in yesterday, nor can I worry about tomorrow. God has given this day as a gift to me. What I do with it is my gift to him.

So I think I'll go to tonight's meeting. Maybe I'll hear West Bill share about the love of his kids. Maybe I'll hear Marty and Patty share about their three years in recovery that started with Alcoholics Anonymous being brought into their prison. Maybe I'll hear Steve, with his old Big Book, share about the wonders of a God of his understanding.

Maybe I'll finally hear that new woman share for the very first time . . . and I certainly don't want to miss that! Maybe I'll hear you. And I'll be able to stay sober one more day listening to experience, strength, and hope being shared, because that's what happened when I went to last night's meeting!

Lowell N.
Ashton, Idaho
July 2005

A Solution for Teenagers

I HAD LOTS OF DOUBTS and concerns when I first came in. Would these people really accept me? Did these rooms full of cigarette smoke and coffee really have something to offer me? Did the program really work?

Being the youngest kid in the room (only thirteen at the time) I spent many nights in the back corner all alone with no one to talk to. I heard many wisecracks such as "My sobriety is three times your age!" Confused and hurt by these comments, I spent nights tossing and turning in bed with thoughts running through my head: Do these people care? Am I too young to sober up? But one question really stuck in my mind: Where were all the other kids?

After about six months, I was sitting in the back of the room with a friend during a business meeting when the thought came to both of us that we should a have a meeting for teenagers in AA. We brought the idea up with our group's steering committee and we were asked to make a proposal at the next business meeting. We wrote up the proposal, got some people to vote in favor of it, and at the present time we have a growing number of kids who attend.

I really stress the importance of teenager meetings in AA because I know when I came into the Fellowship, I just needed a sober individual my age to talk to. I've been to many meetings where my friends' parents or my parents' friends were in attendance. I sometimes felt as if my anonymity was at stake and I was afraid to speak about how I felt on certain issues.

Having a teenager meeting allows teenagers who are new to AA to see that there are people to support them and that there is life after sobriety.

Remember when you first came into AA and you were yearning for someone to share your feelings with?

Kenny K.
Richardson, Texas
January 1997

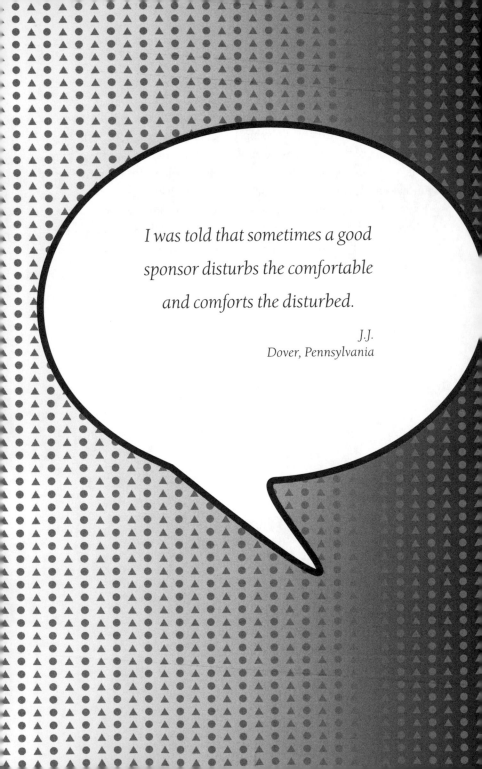

Section Three: **SPONSORSHIP, THE HEART OF AA**

Sponsorship – The Heart of AA

I guess it all really depends on whom you ask and on when you ask it: What is the most important job in AA? While I certainly don't wish to diminish the importance of our many "jobs" in AA, I am grateful for this opportunity to express my opinion.

There exists little doubt in my mind, or heart, that sponsorship has been, and continues to be, the most important job in AA for me. I also believe there are some valid criteria for a good sponsor. First of all, my sponsor has sufficient time in AA, with good quality sobriety. I've also been taught that the best way to be a good sponsor is to be a good sponsee. My sponsor has a sponsor. His sponsor has a sponsor. The people that I have respect for, with good quality sobriety and longevity, use sponsors themselves.

I further believe that if I am able to manipulate my sponsor, then I really don't have one. I'm glad to say I have never been able to manipulate this man. I also know my sponsor is the most active and positive member of AA that I've ever known. He has always been a good example. He has always been gentle but firm, firm but gentle.

At first my sponsor provided AA basics: how to stay away from that first drink one day at a time, the importance of going to meetings on a regular basis, the necessity of a home group, trying to carry the message on a daily basis.

He has always been there for me. I've shared all of my life story with him over time, and he has always shared his with me. He can and does keep a confidence. As a result, I finally was able to put trust in another human being. I've been taught that trust is the very basis of faith. Without good sponsorship, I would have no faith in a Higher Power today. I wouldn't even be sober.

I haven't always liked this man but I have always respected him. And I haven't always followed his suggestions or advice. As a result, I've made many errors and mistakes. Yet, he has always allowed me the right to be wrong. His "able example" of love, tolerance, patience, and kindness has taught me more about what my Higher Power is all about than I could have learned in any other way.

I've been sponsored into service. He taught me that "service is gratitude made visible." As a result, I've not only stayed sober but have found in the process a way of living infinitely better than any way I've ever known.

I found out after the fact that I didn't choose him. Rather, he made himself available to me as a friend. He's turned out to be the best friend I've ever had.

Today, I go to meetings looking for the newcomer. I try to quietly sidle up to him, and make myself available as a friend. We exchange phone numbers and get together for coffee. I try to give it away, as it's been so freely given to me. What a deal!

I believe Bill W. and Dr. Bob sponsored each other out of necessity in the beginning. Today, of course, we enjoy a Fellowship which owes its ever-increasing membership of recovering alcoholics (unprecedented in human history) to the well-wishers and combined efforts of many outside agencies and services, as well as many professionals. To these folks, we surely owe a debt of gratitude.

Yet, the heart of AA remains the same, thank God, when one alcoholic reaches out to another, and we find that we can do together what none of us could do alone.

Jim T.
Aberdeen, South Dakota
September 1991

Learning to Love

I live in a suburb of Chicago, and I'm twenty-four years old. By the grace of God, I've been sober for ten years. Sometimes that feels like forever, and other times like just yesterday. I still have a lot to learn.

Nobody in my immediate family is an alcoholic, so I really have nobody to blame for my disease. Although I was born with a very mild form of cerebral palsy, it doesn't affect my lifestyle at all. Most people don't even recognize the problem until I tell them, yet as a child I used this disability as an excuse for why I was never good enough. Today I do not use this condition as an excuse for my alcoholism either. As I grew up, I had no self-esteem or any problem-solving ability. I started to feel more and more like an outsider. Why should anyone else care for me when I didn't even like myself? So when alcohol came into my life, I took to it very fast. I never really crossed the line into alcoholism – I started out past that line. At that time, I saw my life as being really bad: now, looking back, I know I was fortunate that I had a relatively high bottom. It doesn't mean I can forget that pain. Whenever there is a shooting at a school being covered by the media, my reaction is just like everyone else's. I'm shocked at today's youth. Then I have to remember that it could have been me. I remember being in grade school and carrying around weapons, or having parties in the eighth grade where people would be firing off handguns in the backyard. When I was ten years old, I broke a classmate's neck. I was on a first-name basis with the youth cop in my town because my friends and I had had so many encounters with him. All in all, my life was anything but normal and I've earned my seat at the tables of AA. I wish I could tell a very elaborate bottoming-out story, but the truth is much more simple. I got caught drinking at the age of fourteen. A forty-five minute evaluation turned into a thirty-six day alcohol/drug rehabilitation stay. It was there that I decided I wanted to stay sober for the rest of my life. It seemed easy enough at the time!

Then I went to my first meeting. I looked around and didn't see anybody who looked like me. There were men and women there who were older than my parents. They started talking about DWIs and losing things like spouses, houses, and jobs. These were things I'd never even had, let alone lost. I knew two things: I didn't want to live the way I was living and these people had what I wanted. Nonetheless, here I felt I was an outsider again. As usual, I did everything in the world to try and fit in. I'd exaggerate my drinking history to a point that nobody in his right mind would believe it. Since puberty was still kicking in, my voice was higher than most of the men's voices, so during the Lord's Prayer I'd try and make my voice sound lower than it really was. These deceptions were quite ridiculous, but my fellow AAs tolerated them because they truly cared about me.

When it came time to find a sponsor, I decided to show everyone my "independence" and chose the most outrageous man I could find, someone I was sure my parents wouldn't approve of. Doug was an unemployed street musician and he didn't stay sober much past my first anniversary. One of the things Doug did do was to get me started on the Steps right away. I will never forget Doug for giving me the gift of the Twelve Steps.

During my first few years, everything was new to me. School became awkward for several reasons: first, because I was attending it on a regular basis. Second, because I was changing my playgrounds and playmates. Right about this time I met a few people outside meetings. They weren't alcoholics, but rather members of Alateen. Even though I never attended one of their meetings or even had the required membership, these kids still took me under their wing. I can't explain how grateful I am to those young kids for being my safety net at such places as school.

During the same weekend as my one-year anniversary one of these kids killed himself. This tragedy took hold of me very intensely. I was feeling scared, confused, sad, angry, and a dozen other emotions, all at the same time. I had no idea how to handle it, so I went to an AA meeting that night and explained what I was going through. A man sitting next to me didn't have anything wise to tell me – he didn't say anything at all. He just put his hand on my shoulder, and it was as if a burden was lifted from me. I knew then that I didn't have to go through this alone. This man's small gesture meant the world to me.

I learned two very important things that day: I will never have to go through anything alone in AA. Also I realized I'd had my first spiritual experience. I understood then that not only did people care about me, but I cared for other people. The fact that I mourned for this friend proved that

I cared. Before I came into AA, I didn't love myself and I didn't love anybody else. I know that this kind of growth, this learning to love, could never have been accomplished on my own. This growth had to be a gift from God. These two realizations led me to everything I know about God. The "God as I understand him" really doesn't exist, because I don't understand him any better than I did when I first came into the Fellowship. There are, however, two things that I have learned: one, God is always with me; I never have to be alone again. Two, God has a plan for me. I may not know what that plan is, but he has a plan.

After a few years of sobriety, some of the teenage members of AA were asking me to be their sponsor. This meant only one thing to me: I'm the boss. My ego soared. Then these kids started coming to me with their problems. A lot of these problems were way too much for me to comprehend. There were so many of them. These sponsees would ask me for rides to meetings, ask me about what to do about an abusive parent, ask me about sex issues, and ask me about a hundred different other things that I had no idea how to handle. I would think to myself, I've been sober this long, I should have more answers. One by one, each of the kids that I was working with would "go back out there." I felt crushed and inadequate. I thought that if I was a better sponsor, they wouldn't have taken a drink. I didn't look at the statistics: only a few of us make it as teenagers. I wanted to save everyone, and I took it very hard when I couldn't.

As a result I got burned out on Twelfth Step work. While it is true that I can't keep it if I don't give it away, I also learned I can't give it away if I don't have it. Today I approach working with new people in AA very differently. Instead of raising my ego, the experience makes me more humble. I allow myself to admit that I don't have all of the answers and I explain this to my sponsees. Being a sponsor also forces me to reconsider things that I just take for granted. A matter such as "faith" (a concept that I have very little trouble with today) becomes expanded when I try to explain it to someone for the first time. Just today, I had to look something up in the Big Book that I wanted a sponsee to learn about. I am not afraid to say the traumatic "I don't know" and try to direct them to someone who might.

There have been times when I start to feel sorry for myself. Not so much because I am not able to drink, but for always having to be responsible for my actions. I think to myself that teenagers and young people are supposed to do stupid things, and because I have a program, I can't! At times I've wished that I wasn't a member of AA. Happily, these thoughts don't last as long as they used to.

In AA I have experienced a lot. I have had many firsts. I got my driver's license. I graduated from high school. I got my first car, and I totaled my first car. I got my first job, and I got fired for the first time. I fell in love for the first time, and I got my heart broken for the first time. Each time I went through something new, I had people in AA to go through it with me. I became a fire-fighter, a black belt in judo, a scuba diver, and most of all, a man. I've made many friends in the Fellowship and shared many experiences. I've gone on vacations, weddings, bachelor parties, and even gone skydiving. I am experiencing life to the fullest. I know that would not have been possible without the AA program to guide my life by.

Keven P.
Elk Grove Village, Illinois
June 2000

The Kid Who Came In from the Cold

I was first taken to AA by a clergyman in 1964. I did not want to be an AA member or quit drinking, but I did want to be reunited with the family. I was twenty-five years old.

At first, I attended meetings regularly. I read the Big Book. The family and I were reunited. Life began to get good again. It's unfortunate that some of us equate physical well-being and getting back on our feet with mental and spiritual soundness. I began to attend meetings less and less.

51

I began to say to myself, "You know, you might have been a little rash in coming to AA so soon." Hardly anyone was under forty, much less twenty-six.

Being the only Hispanic, I decided alcoholism was an Irish disease. I didn't qualify.

There were those also who were only too ready to show me the way out by their comments. They were the men who sat around the club and told war stories about their drinking. "Boy," they would say, "I spilled more whiskey on my tie than you ever drank." Or, "Kid. How many times did you go to jail? Do you still have your family? You do! Well, what are you doing here?" Then, they would hit you with the killer. "It's a good thing that you didn't have to go through what we had to suffer, Kid." No question about it. They were the "real" men. When they said "Kid," and gave me that disdainful stare, I knew that I did not measure up, that down deep inside I was a closet wimp.

I took a nearly full-time job in the evenings, and when friends came to invite me to go with them to meetings, I declined. Oh, certainly I would plan to attend some of the functions once in a while. I could be a source of inspiration to all those less fortunate than I, which was nearly everyone from my point of view. I was different. I would not drink again. I knew that I was an undiscovered natural resource whose time had not yet come. "Drink again? Why, that is utterly out of the question." Perhaps, in the past, I had been a bit bizarre on occasion, but that's expected when a great mind is subjected to the mundane trivialities of life such as having to work for a living. I was the most surprised one of all when I got drunk.

Something that rarely fails to impress nearly every newcomer is what my sponsor calls "the magic of AA." We meet clean, well-dressed people who seem genuinely warm and friendly. We find firm handshakes and compassionate hearts. Here, at last, are people who understand exactly how we have felt. They give of themselves unselfishly, offering to take us to meetings and giving us their phone numbers. They tell us that they care. And most importantly, they say, "Come back. We need you." No matter how insincere you might be when you arrive, you cannot help but be impressed by the love and acceptance that you find. An overwhelming sense of hope is experienced, perhaps for the first time, as we are welcomed into the Fellowship.

If, like me, you happen to drink again and are fortunate enough to return to AA, you may find that there is a little less hope and a little less of the magic than you first experienced. I was one of those who bounced in and out of AA for quite some time. I was never sober for more than three weeks at any one time and that only occurred once. Each time I returned, there was less and less of the magic.

There were all those who had gotten sober since I had first come in. I especially hated them. As time went on, I began to notice a few things. I noticed that when I got up to get my tenth "white chip" of the month, the applause wasn't quite as enthusiastic as I remembered it. It occurred to me that no one had offered their phone number to me for quite some time. Whenever one of those newly sober members rushed up to save me, their sponsor called them away.

It wasn't that I lacked a desire to stop drinking. Each time I returned, I returned with all the sincerity I could muster. The problem was that I had lost the ability to control my drinking and was not able to stay sober on my own resources. Those of us who are sober sometimes forget that lack of success does not necessarily mean lack of sincerity.

There comes a time when nothing matters anymore. There was no magic left. It had all dissolved in a sea of alcohol. I was coming to AA because I had nowhere else to go. I had run out of alternatives. It was December of 1968. The family was gone. So was the house, the car, and everything else. I was living in what had once been chicken coops and were now "remodeled" for people such as myself. I was alone. I wandered in and out of AA almost mechanically, getting a white chip if they offered it. At the time, I weighed about 100 pounds. I couldn't sleep. I couldn't eat anything that would stay down. I was impotent. I was so sick, mentally as well as physically, that I could not maintain a conversation with anyone. After a few minutes, most people just got up and left. It was at this time that I went to a meeting with a man whom I had asked to be my sponsor during one of my brief periods of sobriety. He never gave up on me.

That night, when the group secretary did the chip system, I got another white chip. It was January 20, 1969. I have not gotten another one since. The point of this story is that there is no such thing as a "hopeless slipper." There are "slippers" that we label "hopeless" when we don't want to bother with them anymore. My first sponsor never gave up on me. He knew that repeatedly getting drunk did not mean that I had no desire to stop drinking. Sincerity of desire cannot be judged by amount of success. I should know that as well as anyone, yet, in sobriety, I too have been guilty, at times, of casting the same judgment upon others. How quickly we forget! Part of the magic of AA is that the Fellowship, like the "loving God who presides over us all," never gives up hope for the suffering alcoholic. My first sponsor knew this. He knew that unconditional love is what often makes the difference between living and dying for the man or woman who seeks shelter in Alcoholics Anonymous. He knew that when we gave up all hope for those still "out there," we had lost the magic of AA ourselves. And, we had lost it sober.

C.C.
West Palm Beach, Florida
September 1986

Thank You, Old-Timers

When I found AA, I felt as if I was 200 years old. I had hip-hugger jeans (which were all I owned), tight-fitting shirt, and long, sexy (I thought) brown hair. I was as skinny as a bean pole but thought I weighed 400 pounds (I now know that was all the guilt I was carrying around).

Inside, I was dead. I felt like an absolute zero and that my life was over. The lady my mother had taught me to be and the God she had taught me to believe in were both long gone, like ashes thrown to the wind. I was totally defeated and scared to death.

The people in the AA meeting room moved around, laughing, talking, and having fun. I knew someone was going to touch me any minute, and I would explode into a million pieces. While I was feeling all this, I was also sizing up this group I had fallen into because I had no place else left to go. I saw older people, with graying hair or no hair at all. I thought, "Oh no! This is what I've been running from all my life – authority and older people trying to run my life."

While I was still in this frame of mind, one of the older members, a gray-haired, attractive (I did give her that much) lady, came up to me and told me she would be my temporary sponsor. I thanked her but wondered to myself, "What is she talking about?" Thank God, I filed this information away. Little did I know how desperately I would need it.

My start in AA was very shaky. Looking back, I am scared when I think how shaky it really was. You see, I landed right in the middle of some young people who, unfortunately, were quite often offended by the old-timers' suggestions, and the advice "Stick with the winners" would throw them into a rebellious frenzy. It was also brought to their attention that AA needs no specialization by age, that we are all in this together. That, too, they weren't willing to hear.

After three months of this beginning in AA, I found myself very confused and very uncomfortable. I knew something was wrong, but I didn't know what. I knew I had to change if I wanted to live, but I didn't know how to go about it. So God, in His infinite wisdom, helped me to recall the information I had been given three months earlier: Sponsor! It hit me. I first approached my sponsor out of total desperation. She helped me get through my confusion, and I made a new start in AA.

The new course I had to take was not an easy one. It meant leaving behind the only young people in AA that I knew at that time. It meant that

I had to be willing to go to any length to get what I so desperately wanted — what those beautiful older members had. It meant ridicule from my peers every so often. It meant that for the first time in my life, I had to be willing to listen and take directions from the people I had rebelled against for so long. Often, it meant being a fifth wheel and wondering if I would ever have friends my own age who were trying to live this program the way AA suggests we live it.

Some of the hurt subsided, because these older members must have known how I felt, and they took me under their wing and loved me until I could again stand on my own two feet. Today, I know no age difference. I have friends of all ages, and my best friend is in her fifties.

Thank you, old-timers, for my life.

R. B.
Chapel Hill, North Carolina
January 1978

We've Got What You Need

In the early days of my sobriety, I asked this guy sitting next to me at a meeting, "Do you think I'm too young to be alcoholic?"

"Oh, I don't know," he said. "What are you: thirty-four, thirty-five maybe?"

"What!" I shouted. "I'm twenty-three."

"Honey," he said emphatically, "you're in the right place."

Indeed I was and I am.

Shortly after that, I asked my sponsor if she thought I was "too young to be in AA." Since I hadn't had any luck with "too young to be alcoholic," I tried "too young for AA."

"Kay," she said, "you are a fortunate young woman — we've got what you need." She paused a minute and then said, "Let's get with it, huh?"

And I "got with it" — May 22, 1962.

I had no idea how to live without alcohol. I didn't know how to work, cook, eat, talk, care about myself or anyone else. I was carrying around a load of guilt that was killing me, and I hated myself and everybody else.

AA taught me how to live my life without taking a drink by teaching me how to live the Twelve Steps. It gave me an understanding of the disease I was living with and how it manifested itself in all areas of my being: physically, mentally, and spiritually. And it gave me a Higher Power other than booze.

Because the desire for a drink didn't leave me for a long time, my fellow alcoholics spent hours and hours and days and days talking to me about the AA program at meetings, in all-night coffee shops, in the park, in the zoo, at the beach — anywhere and everywhere, they were there.

They talked about every aspect of the Twelve Steps and Twelve Traditions, the principles, the disease, sponsorship, Twelfth Step calls, establishing conscious contact with a Higher Power, the Fourth and Fifth Steps, and things I should and shouldn't do to stay sober.

Sometimes they talked so much I thought my ears would fall off. But I knew they cared and I was staying sober so I knew they were right. I loved the way they talked to me: right up front, no games, no foolishness, just the truth.

These sober alcoholics gave me things I never knew existed — love, time, acceptance, honesty, fun, laughter, breakfast, showing up, coffee and doughnuts, and me.

So how do I share my glorious gift of sobriety with young people? How do I reach out to them? What form does my Twelfth Step call take in 1996?

I attend four or five meetings a week. I am visible, verbal, and available. I celebrate my anniversaries to demonstrate "eternal vigilance" when it comes to staying sober. I have a home group.

When called on to talk at meetings, I talk about my AA experiences: how the Steps work, on a day-to-day basis, to help me live a sober life. I talk about my Higher Power.

57

I hang around after my home group meetings and fire off my one-liners: you did good, come back, do you have a sponsor, just don't drink, hang in, hang tough, here's my phone number, call me anytime. And if they call, that's great; if not, that's okay too. I don't have everybody's message but if we keep them coming back somebody will.

Sometimes I reach out aggressively, as I did with one young woman I sponsor. I first saw her at an early morning meeting where she was reading to us from a book she had borrowed from her church library. She did this a couple of times before I asked her if she would stay and talk to me after the meeting.

She was sober about a month and had no sponsor. When I asked if she would like me to be her temporary sponsor until she found a permanent one, she said, "Yes." She is now sober four years, and we are still sponsee and sponsor.

Another woman I sponsor is an alcoholic and drug addict. When she first asked me to be her sponsor, I said, "No." She cried so much I said, "Let me talk to my sponsor in Louisiana." My sponsor told me that I could certainly go through the Steps with her, share my experience, strength, and hope as an alcoholic, and be there when she needed me. We agreed that we would talk only about alcohol and she would attend NA for her drug addiction. She listens, she follows directions, and she is sober two and a half years.

The third woman I am sponsoring is twenty-three and has over two years of sobriety. Two statements she says she hates to hear are: "Oh my goodness, you're so young," and "You're only twenty?" She says these statements make her feel as if she couldn't make a decision about being an alcoholic and she couldn't know the pain and devastation of acute alcoholism.

For my sake, as well as the well-being of the women I sponsor, I stay within what I know. I tell them I'm not a mother, sister, favorite aunt, therapist, counselor, guru, spiritual advisor, AA authority, and sometimes not even a friend. I'm just another drunk who didn't drink and didn't die for thirty-three years and I know how to stay sober one day at a time in AA. I share my experience, strength, and hope.

Also in order not to cloud the issue of getting sober and staying sober in AA, I stay away from terms such as relate, relationships, co-dependency, inner child, dysfunctional, adult child of an alcoholic, drugs, the Bible, etc., etc., etc. It is my experience that these concepts get in the way of learning the AA way of life, and quite honestly I don't know what they mean in relation to sobriety.

Each generation has its own unique problems; times change, people change, and language may change. But the disease of alcoholism does not change. It always kills. In thirty-three years of sobriety I have not seen this change.

The resolution of active alcoholism is death or AA.

One time when someone had pulled the "You're so young" routine on my twenty-year-old sober alcoholic, she asked, "Where in the Big Book does it say you have to be forty or fifty to stay drunk all day? Where is it written there is an age requirement? How old do you have to be to die from drinking?" "Yo! Gimme respect," she said.

Yo! kid. You'll get it from me as it was given to me. Young people get my attention and my understanding for what they're trying to do to stop drinking and change their lives. I love them because they know they have a problem with alcohol, and they have the guts to do something about it. Alcoholism is not an old person's disease. Nobody gets to AA by mistake.

Young people need the same acceptance, love, understanding, consistency and time we give anyone who walks through the doors of AA for the first time or after a slip or after twenty-five slips. I hope by our words, deeds and presence we make it known we are willing to give them what they need.

The AA I knew back in 1962 told me, "Come on in, we've been waiting for you, we've got what you need." The AA I know today says, "Come on in, we've been waiting for you, we've got what you need."

If old-timers don't tell young people this, who will?
Pass it on.

Kay P.
Beaumont, Texas
February 1996

The Gift of Time

I was sober about eight months when Charlie began to call. I met him at a young people's conference. (What was he doing there?)

He would call me every morning and ask, "What kind of day are you going to have?"

"An excellent day," I would reply (even though I didn't really believe it). When he asked "Why?" I would reply, "Because I am not going to drink today."

Charlie would call me regardless of whether or not I was working that day. It made no difference if I wanted to sleep in or had the day off. Most days he would call in the evening to see how my day went.

I was twenty-three years old, fresh out of a long-term treatment facility and I was on my own in a strange town. My face was badly scarred from my last car accident and my insides were badly scarred from a life of drinking, fear, and hate.

Charlie was in his sixties, had false teeth, wore string ties and smiled all the time. He was known as the "Official Handshaker" and would stand by the door at meetings and shake hands with everyone. He wouldn't leave me alone.

He and my sponsor formed a sober tag-team. They made me get involved and stand at the meeting door to shake hands. When it was time to share and I hadn't raised my hand, I would get a tap or an elbow. I eventually learned that Charlie was my sponsor's sponsor, or my "grand-sponsor."

They gave me their time. They would listen to me. Charlie would speak of stories that I didn't really understand until later (and to be honest, some I still don't understand). I often lost patience but they didn't care.

It gradually dawned on me that these men loved me. They would make me laugh and made light of my problems. One time as I complained about their uncaring attitude, Charlie told me, "If I didn't love you and think you were worth it, I wouldn't spend my time with you."

I began to learn the difference between my understanding of love and "AA" love. It isn't always "warm fuzzies" and kid gloves and pats on the back. Sometimes it is the truth. I was told that sometimes a good sponsor disturbs the comforted and comforts the disturbed.

I have now been sober almost four years. I try to stay active and enthusiastic in AA. My life is wonderful compared to the hell I used to live in. I have a good job. I recently got engaged and got a dog. Charlie died over a year ago – I tried to shake everyone's hand at his memorial service. I cried a lot, but I feel as though he is still with me.

Charlie (and AA) have left me with an obligation. I fulfilled my obligation to the treatment center I attended when I paid my bill. I no longer feel a sense of obligation to my rehab. I do feel a sense of obligation to Alcoholics Anonymous. I can "pay back" AA by trying to be there for the next person to come through the door. I can give myself and my time. I can stay active and pay attention to the Traditions. I'm not perfect and I will never balance the ledger, but I can keep trying. After all, someone was there for me.

J. J.
Dover, Pennsylvania
June 1991

The Best Listeners

I have bored my sponsor to tears and she has never once complained. She just let me go on and on.

Since I myself sponsor several women, I've been on both sides of the telephone, hearing the same stories over and over again until the days turn into months and then become years of sharing. This sponsoring business requires patience.

To my own dear sponsor I have repeated the trials of my marriage breakup so many times that I bored even myself with it. She never once gave me the feeling that I was annoying her. In my attempt to stay sober, I've confessed my deepest secrets in a Fifth Step to her and admitted my drink signals when they came. She was always available to listen to me anytime I called.

I've heard a number of Fifth Steps in my own living room and across my kitchen table — stories of alcoholism, dependency, shameful past experiences, and enormous pain.

The process of one alcoholic confiding in another has without a doubt saved my life. Nowhere else have I ever found such devotion and understanding as with AA sponsoring.

Who else, other than an AA member, would accept a phone call in the middle of a busy work day to listen to: "I'm sorry to call you at work, but I'm terrified at this moment. I don't think I'll make it through the day without a drink. What should I do?"

What is most miraculous in this scenario is the fact that this person had someone to call instead of picking up a drink, and that is how it works.

We AAs are the best listeners in the world — that is, when we're not talking!

Linda M.
Maspeth, New York
May 1998

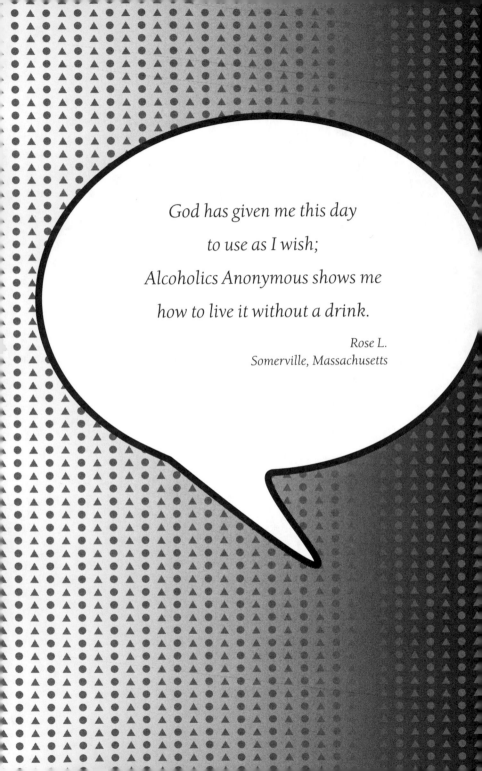

God has given me this day

to use as I wish;

Alcoholics Anonymous shows me

how to live it without a drink.

Rose L.
Somerville, Massachusetts

Section Four: **IT WORKS IF YOU WORK IT**

Changes for the Better

My parents were very young when I was born – too young to take care of themselves, let alone me. During my childhood I came to believe that drinking was okay; I thought it was normal. I was an only child and often drank to fend off the loneliness. My whole family was tied up in drugs and alcohol. My father and mother got divorced, and a few years later my father tried to kill himself under the influence of drugs. That didn't stop me from drinking.

I quit school and started drinking on a daily basis. I hung out with the wrong crowd. I stayed out all night, went to bars, got into fights, and got arrested. I got into so much trouble that the courts gave me a sentence of one year in jail, suspended. I was put on probation for two years, and my probation officer quickly noticed my alcoholism. She threatened me with ten days in jail if I didn't admit myself to a treatment center.

In the treatment center, I realized that my world was falling apart. I was no longer living, I was struggling. I knew I couldn't go on that way much longer. I learned a lot about the disease of alcoholism and was introduced to the Fellowship of Alcoholics Anonymous. That treatment center was a major stepping stone in my life. Through the program I found a new freedom and a new happiness. AA is a way of life today, because for me to drink is to die and I want very much to live.

The Promises say I can be restored to a "normal" way of life – unfortunately I had no normal way of life to be restored to. I'm still learning how to live happy, joyous, and free. In order to be those things, I must work the program to the best of my ability, just the way it has been laid out. I cannot fix it to my liking. I must surrender myself totally. I've turned my will over to the care of a Higher Power whom I choose to call God. I've accepted the gift of grace.

Willingness, awareness, acceptance, and honesty are the keys to my emotional sobriety. I'm willing to go to any lengths to keep my sobriety.

I have the willingness to make changes — and I really have changed for the better. I'm honest today; I need not put on an act for people to like me. I'm not afraid to let my skeletons out of their closets. I am learning to love myself as well as to love others. I learn this by being open and honest, by sharing in groups. I share my experience, strength, and hope, and my fears, doubts, and insecurities. By this I may be able to help a fellow alcoholic.

All I need to do is continue to go to AA meetings and stick with the winners. I want that sparkle in my eye, that skip in my step that they have. So I've joined a group and gotten involved as much as possible by helping to set up the meetings and by going on commitments. I keep in contact with sober people every day. I have a sponsor and I try to stay away from sick situations. I can enjoy healthy relationships. I can love and be loved. I set goals in my recovery and stick with them. I have so much to give and so much more to receive. I can believe in myself and I'm grateful for the beautiful people God has put in my life.

I get on my knees in the morning and ask for God's will, not mine, to be done for the day. I return the gift of grace at night. I kneel at my bedside and thank God for all that he has helped me with. I go to sleep and look forward to another day. Before sobriety, I never honestly looked forward to a new day. God has given me this day to use as I wish; Alcoholics Anonymous shows me how to live it without a drink.

Rose L.
Somerville, Massachusetts
September 1995

Connecting the Dots

My first drunk was when I was twelve years old. My friends and I went to a little store a mile away and stole pints of Mad Dog 20/20. My pint was of the Plum Supreme variety. I remember drinking most of it and passing out on the bicycle trail. My friends had to carry me back to our fort. I woke up in the morning as drunk as when I passed out. I was muddy and I couldn't find my shoes. I stumbled across the street; on the way a friend stopped me and told me not to go home, that I was too drunk. I went anyway. My mom was doing her face in the bathroom and I tried to pass by quietly to get to my bedroom. I would have given anything to go to sleep. She saw me and asked me why my lips were stained purple. My answer: grape Kool-Aid. She immediately knew I was drunk, and proceeded to hold me in a cold shower. She wouldn't let me sleep and made me go to soccer practice, where I suffered badly. By the next day, I couldn't wait to do it again.

Shortly after age twelve I began smoking cigarettes and using drugs on a regular basis. I drank and partied hard, mostly on weekends. By the age of sixteen I'd run away at least four times. I was leaving school early to wash dishes and lived with a high school buddy paying rent in his grandma's basement because my stepdad and I did not get along. I went home off and on.

Then I met a young lady and we started going out. I put her through hell. I had run-ins with the police on five occasions. I was also very angry. One time she was driving me to a doctor's appointment and when we couldn't find the office, I shattered the windshield with my fist. She lied to cover for me.

My mom worked at my high school cafeteria and she'd feed me. My girlfriend was in most of my classes and she'd do my homework and drag me out of bed every morning. I was worthless most of the time with terrible hangovers. I read one book in the fifth grade and did a book report on it every year. I graduated from high school five minutes before graduation with a fraction of a credit over what I needed. I didn't earn my diploma: my mother and my girlfriend earned it.

By this time I was $3,000 in debt to a drug dealer. A guy with a gun climbed in my window and was going to take my life; my dad intervened. I gave him the truck my dad had bought for me. Shortly after graduation, I lost my second job due to drinking. I was fixing cars and was so sick from drinking that I got to work (usually late), got my first car of the day, then passed out in the back seat. I would go on two-hour test drives in order to get drugs and alcohol. I hocked my tools or lost them. I had and lost two more jobs after that. During this time, my girlfriend's parents had me over to their house. They sat me down and asked me if I thought they liked me. I said yes. They said, "Well, Greg, we don't like you. We barely know you and what little we do know, we don't like. But we want to give you a chance." They invited me over for dinner the following week. I couldn't stay sober long enough to even go back there. After five years, my girlfriend was finally tired of babysitting and she left me.

This tore me up terribly, but I couldn't drink enough to eliminate the feelings; I hated that. Alcohol began not working. My roommate stocked shelves at a grocery store at night. I hadn't paid rent in two months and would sneak in at night and steal what I could find to survive. I couldn't work anymore. On my last drunk before I asked for help, I walked two miles to my mom's, broke in, and stole the fullest half-gallon I could find. It happened to be peppered vodka she used for cooking. I drank it all and lay on the floor with the barrel of a .22 rifle in my mouth, contemplating pulling the trigger. But I couldn't handle the thought of my roommate finding me there after all I'd done to him, so I picked up the phone and called the treatment center my dad had gone to seven years before. They talked to me for a long time. The next day I went to see my mom and two days later I was in out-patient treatment. The night before going into treatment I had to beg my older stepbrother to loan me a nickel and go to the store to buy my last forty ounces of cheap beer. He did it reluctantly. That was my last drink.

I didn't know AA existed, but the treatment center told me I had to go. I went to my first meeting when I was twenty years old at a fellowship hall where there was a dance afterwards. It was a Friday night and I was very excited. The secretary of the meeting was seventeen years old and had been sober for nine months. I was blown away. He gave me his phone number and told me to keep coming back. I went to the dance afterward and one girl asked me to dance. I knew right then that I would marry her and we would live together forever. Well, I never saw her again. I was a little delusional!

I went to a meeting every day at this hall. I began washing cars on a car lot. At two months sober I was called to go to school for a large company where I'd applied for a job. It was for two months without pay and no job guarantee. I took it. I had to beg my parents to take me in for two months. They reluctantly gave me the garage apartment. I did well in school but didn't get the job. I was severely disappointed. I moved in with my old drinking partners which was not comfortable. While there I hit bottom in sobriety. I wanted to drink after eight months of meetings, but I knew to drink was to die. Yet I felt like I was going to die if I didn't get a drink. I was sitting in the fellowship hall kitchen flipping through my "Twelve and Twelve" and Big Book and looking for the answer, but I couldn't find it. I looked up and I saw Ken W. and told him I wanted to die. He asked me if I was ready to follow directions yet and willing to go to any length. I said, "Yes, finally." He wrote on a napkin what I was to read and write for thirty days. The directions were very easy and specific. He told me that if I missed one day to start over, and if I missed two days he wouldn't sponsor me any longer. This was the first day of the wonderful life I have today.

I used to whine and snivel so much in meetings that the first time I had anything positive to say, I was given a standing ovation. Until that moment I hadn't been able to see how negative and angry I had been. I was quite set back. But I followed all the directions for thirty days and amazing things began to happen. I was asked to chair my first meeting at a group, which I later chose as my home group. I began to act as secretary at a Saturday night speakers' meeting. I had to get two speakers each week and show up every Saturday at 7:00 P.M.

When Ken W. became my sponsor, I wasn't eating regularly and didn't have any income. I asked Ken to feed me and I would pay him back. His answer was, "Get a damn job." I woke up the next morning, hit my knees, and said, "God, I'm going to get a job today. If you will help, that would be great, but even if you don't, I'm going to get one." After five applications, I went to a shop and said, "I'm Greg and I've been sober nine months and I need a job." The man looked at me kind of strangely, but I started the next day. I stayed there three years, and my boss cried when I gave him notice. I again had to ask my parents for a place to stay, but this time they said yes and gave me a bedroom in the house and a key to the front door.

I continued through the Steps and after Step One I had a profound change in attitude. For Step Two, my sponsor had me read *Came to Believe* and told me to pray every morning for sobriety and to thank God at night. I still do this every day. I took Step Three on my knees. I wrote a Fourth Step as best I could, but I didn't feel comfortable doing a Fifth Step with my sponsor because he'd made my resentment list. Instead, I walked into a church to find a priest to share it with. The priest was there with about five people from the meetings I'd been attending. They put me on the spot. I told them what I was trying to do. One lady said I could do it with her husband who was blind. I thought that sounded great! I set up an appointment to see him that night, but I was too squirrely to wait so I ended up going to my sponsor's and did my Fifth Step with him. We found we had much in common. I was a little skimpy in the "we resolutely look for our own mistakes" department. He happily pointed them out to me. I felt so good when I was done. (I've worked Steps Four and Five since then and never gotten the same feeling as my first time.) I went home and read Steps Six and Seven. An hour later I hit my knees and said the Seventh Step prayer. I was a new man. I felt at one with God.

I wrote an Eighth Step list and my sponsor had me start with my little sister, my mom, and my stepfather. Two minutes into my amends, my stepdad got up and walked away; he didn't want to hear it. I finally caught up with him several weeks later. He told me he couldn't understand how I could treat him and others the way I'd done and why I couldn't stop drinking. We talked, and from that day, we have been great friends and love to spend time together.

I paid back most of the money I owed. When I was twelve, my neighbor had gone on vacation and asked me to mow her lawn twice while she was away. I didn't do it but when she came back I collected twenty dollars. Well, ten years later, there I was at the door to pay back the money. She wouldn't take it. While telling her why I was there, she told me her husband was drunk, and I twelfth-stepped him for an hour. She cried and hugged me and I left the twenty dollars (my sponsor said I should have paid a hundred dollars in interest). I continued through most of my amends, including my high school principal whose life I had threatened; she still didn't care to see me.

Eight years later I'm still very active in AA. I serve as a district committee member. I sponsor guys and go to meetings. At our area assembly in 1994 I met the woman who is now my wife and we have a twenty-month-old baby girl. We own a home in the suburbs.

Last year was hard. My sponsor who helped me so much lost his life. I miss him. Our oldest home group member also passed on. Two other close friends died as a result of alcoholism. I'm so grateful to be blessed with sobriety and happiness. My sponsor always told me to maintain an attitude of gratitude and not to forget where I'd come from and I'd never have to go back.

Greg P.
Brier, Washington
May 1998

Peace at Last

I grew up in a violent alcoholic home, and although I don't believe that environment turned me into an alcoholic, I can't deny that it played a part in my alcoholic drama. I stole my first drinks from my mother and grandfather as soon as I was tall enough to snatch their glasses from the dining-room table. I loved the attention and excitement as my mother yelled and chased me, trying to retrieve her brandy. I remember the burning sensation sliding down my throat, through my chest, and into my belly. I felt invincible.

As a child, I was full of anger and fought with my classmates on a regular basis. And when I learned that the violence and insanity I lived with at home were not normal, that knowledge fed my rage. I got into so many fistfights that the few friends I had grew frightened of me and stopped talking to me.

I was thirteen the first time I poured my own tumbler of booze. I was home alone, and I drank the whole thing. What happened next was magic. My anger began to subside. I didn't care about Mom's drinking or Dad's violence — or anything else, for that matter. I became numb, and I thought it was the best thing that had ever happened to me.

The next time I was home alone I repeated the experiment. Soon I began taking liquor to school in my book bag. Sure, I drank more than I intended sometimes, but at least I had stopped fighting. I didn't get angry as long as I could drink, and I got my friends back.

Less than a year after my first drunk, my best friend asked me to go to a meeting of Alcoholics Anonymous. She pointed out that I drank too much, that I drank whenever I was alone, and that when I wasn't alone, I refused to share my alcohol. Drinking had become the most important thing to me, and that wasn't normal. I told her, in a not-so-polite way, that I did not have a drinking problem; I had a solution, and my life was better.

But I could not admit to her that it was getting harder to drown the rage. I could ease it, but I couldn't numb it anymore. Sometimes the best I could do was drink until I was physically incapable of acting on my anger. I also had begun to have blackouts and sometimes "came to" in the middle of conversations, not knowing what I was supposed to be talking about.

When I was sixteen, the police arrested a member of my family for domestic violence. The state shuttled me off to a counselor, who quickly ascertained that I had a drinking problem. I loudly insisted that she was wrong; my problem was my violent family. But inside I knew I should probably stop drinking. And since I couldn't get numb anymore anyway, I decided to quit.

I was awfully proud of myself. I bragged about not drinking to anyone who would listen. Okay, so I was sipping here and there, but I figured that didn't count as drinking if I could remember what happened. But as each day passed, I got increasingly angry.

A few weeks later, my rage erupted. I hated myself. I hadn't hit anyone in three years, and I certainly didn't want to behave that way. Consequently, I reasoned that I didn't hit people when I was really drinking, so it seemed I was better off drunk. That kicked off a new cycle: I would stop drinking, become violent, and return to drinking.

Life wasn't all bad. I did have a few successes. I won honors in science, math, and music, became a published author, excelled at varsity sports, and did volunteer work. I was even inducted into the National Honor Society, although I was in a blackout during the induction ceremony. I also had half a dozen serious suicide attempts, several court orders keeping me away from family members, kidney and intestinal malfunctions, violent outbursts, and horrific hallucinations.

After my sixth suicide attempt, I returned to my sip-but-don't-gulp plan for about ninety days. Then on the day I was to graduate from high school, I began sipping in the morning. By the afternoon, I had drunk an entire fifth.

My most vivid memory of the ceremony is of my friend yelling at me for drinking again and then landing a solid right hook on my jaw. That was the beginning of a two-week bender, where I'd come out of one blackout just long enough to get back into another. The next time I stopped, I shook and saw caterpillars everywhere. A few days later, I again attacked someone, this time with a knife and with the intent to kill.

I finally realized that I behaved violently only when I wanted to drink — my drinking was part of the problem. I also realized that I had to ask for help. So I called the counselor the state had sent me to. But when she said she'd take me to an AA meeting, I told her I'd do absolutely anything but that. I told her I was too young; I wouldn't fit in, everyone there would hate me. She disagreed, but suggested the alternative of a treatment center for adolescents. I told her I'd think about it.

I drank that night, and for several nights after that. I didn't know how to stop. Finally, I called her back and entered treatment a week later. I was still hallucinating, but I hadn't had alcohol or a drug for the entire week. At age eighteen, I was the oldest client there. A fifteen-year-old approached me, handed me a Big Book, and told me how much she liked AA meetings.

When the rehab counselors brought me to my first meeting, they assured me that the people in the room were really alcoholics. Immediately, I saw that this was a lie. These people were smiling and laughing and carrying themselves with dignity. They obviously had not experienced my kind of trouble, and I dismissed them as salaried social workers. Then I saw a few people in the room frowning and complaining and some who were downright nuts and decided that if Alcoholics Anonymous was for them, I must be in right place, too.

When I left treatment, I went to ten or twelve AA meetings a week. I got a sponsor, I asked for help on a daily basis, and I continued to stay sober without violent outbursts.

But after a year, I was still full of rage, guilt, and shame. And I was having trouble finishing my Fourth Step, because I was scared of the Fifth: I wasn't interested in sharing my secrets with anyone. I was also contemplating suicide. I had gotten a gun, was holding it in my lap ready to load it, and somehow decided not to use it. Shortly after that, I did my Fifth Step with my sponsor, and she didn't run away. She listened, and then she gently put her hand on my arm, looked me straight in the eye, and said, "Welcome to the human race." I haven't picked up that gun again.

Doing the Sixth and Seventh Steps taught me to ask for help in all areas of my life. But only as I began to make amends did the havoc I had rendered become apparent to me, as did the hope I had of turning it around. Some relationships began to be repaired. My life began to change at a deep, emotional level, and I honestly began to care about — even love — the people around me and myself.

Keeping a Tenth Step journal about my day-to-day life, my relations with other people, and the stuff that still roiled around in my head helped me see patterns in my thoughts and behavior, which I could discuss with my sponsor. And once I began to sit quietly, reflect on what I'd written, and pray, I began to sleep peacefully for the first time in my life.

The Twelfth Step taught me to share my experience with others. So I've set up meetings, sponsored other alcoholics, served as group treasurer, been GSR (General Services representative), and done public information committee work. But one of the most rewarding experiences I've had in sobriety was taking an AA meeting to a local correctional center for women once a week. It's difficult to stay wrapped up in the misery of your own life when an inmate announces she'd like to talk about gratitude. More recently, I've been part of a group that takes meetings to the treatment center I went to in 1989. I see there how young I was when booze took over my life.

Not long ago, I was in a head-on collision with an intoxicated driver. (There but for the grace of God go I.) My leg is badly broken, but the rest of me's intact. It's been a whole new lesson in powerlessness, yet people from AA have been here for me, taking me to doctors and to meetings, bringing me food and hugs, and showing me how to live sober, without violence.

My spirits are good most of the time, and I know my leg will heal. Although I won't be able to return to my job, I'm hoping to return to school and have begun the footwork to achieve that goal. In fact, I've become one of those smiling, happy, and (somewhat) dignified folk who intimidated me so when I first walked into the rooms of AA.

Karen S.
Manchester, New Hampshire
March 2001

Learning the Tools

I'm seventeen years old and a slowly recovering alcoholic. I started drinking to get away from my family and rebel against my parents' expectations and rules. After a few years of being out of the control of my parents, I was placed on probation for unruliness.

When I was sixteen, treatment was the last resort for my rebellious behavior. While in treatment, I learned a lot about the disease of alcoholism and was introduced to Alcoholics Anonymous, but I didn't acquire the tools to stay sober. I went back to my old friends and places, thinking I could deal with them. I stopped going to AA meetings. It took two weeks to get back to where I was before and continue the downhill slide, but at a faster pace.

I entered a long-term treatment center at the age of seventeen. I was shown and began to be aware of my problems with alcohol and what alcohol had cost me. I also became willing to admit that I was powerless over alcohol and that there was a Higher Power and others who could help me.

Today I'm learning the tools and I continue to go to meetings regularly. I talk to my sponsor frequently. I meet and talk to sober people every day, people who are willing to share their experience, strength, and hope with me. I'm very grateful for the people God has put in my life; I don't know where I'd be without all of them. God gives me the gift of each day and I need to accept it as it comes.

Kyle S.
Columbus, Ohio
December 1996

Keep Coming Back — No Matter What

I grew up a pretty lucky kid in a good home in the suburbs of Los Angeles. I feel as if I should start there, saying that I didn't have a poor upbringing, because I've sponsored guys with stories of growing up that have broken my heart. So I know today what a broken home looks like, and I think I can say in confidence today that I was lucky: I was raised well; that was not the cause of my alcoholism.

I do remember, however, the age at which I first started feeling different. I was in kindergarten and couldn't stop tickling the kid next to me. They said I was "hyper" and "wanted attention." When I look back now, I realize this is my first memory of being restless, irritable, and discontented with sitting where I was sitting, being where I was being, anywhere, all the time. I was five years old, and I don't think things changed until I found alcohol.

Before my first drunk, I had grabbed sips of alcohol from my parents' wineglasses, and when I was nine years old or so, I stole a Coors Light out of the refrigerator. I cracked it, took a drink, thought "This tastes horrible," and put it in a drawer in my room to save for later. I took a sip out of it every day until my mom found it about two weeks later. I didn't like that beer, but I felt compelled to finish it.

My first experience getting loaded was actually with marijuana, which I asked my friend Jason if we could smoke. I was thirteen and by then was the smallest kid in a Catholic school of thirty other kids. I was the outcast, the lowest man on the totem pole, and wanted nothing more than to fit in. I thought "smoking out" would make me "a part of" at last. It didn't do that, but it did something else. Lying on the floor of Jason's outdoor deck next to his bong left me thinking, "I want to die like this. I'm going to do this as often as possible every day for the rest of my life."

At first that meant on the weekends in the summer. By the next school year, I began to see the possibilities of being loaded during the day. This was great! I worked at a department store after school, where we would smoke pot two or three times during our six-hour shifts, then get an older coworker to buy us alcohol after closing time. I had definitely arrived. I always had felt as if I were the least in everything, so I set out to become the best of the "burners" as they were called at my high school. By sixteen, I had become quite accomplished. I was reading books on marijuana cultivation, listening to lots of Grateful Dead, and starting in with LSD, nitrous, and alcohol. I had shed my image as the school nerd and was on my way to the burner crown.

The only problem with this was that until then I had been a great student. I got into a competitive private boys' school with a scholarship and was well on my way to the college of my choice. Suddenly, I didn't care about homework, classes — school at all, really. My grades dropped from all As to Cs and Ds. And I couldn't have cared less. I had found a substitute for success in the real world that I liked much better. Unfortunately, my plummeting grades drew a lot of heat, from the school and from my parents. One night I had an especially bad blackout that typified my drinking and using at the time. I went to see a concert with four friends from school, took and drank everything that I could get my hands on, and had to be carried into my house around 2:00 A.M. by my friends. At school the next day, none of them wanted to talk to me, and I couldn't remember a single thing about the night before. Two months later, at sixteen years of age, I found myself walking the streets of Hollywood after midnight by myself, seriously blacked out and debilitated. I was an hour from where I lived, and the friends who had driven me there were gone, lost in our chemical confusion. I have no idea what would have happened if one of my church youth group leaders hadn't found me. He went to college in the area and recognized that I was in serious trouble and needed help. My father was frighteningly silent as he drove me home that night.

The next day I was in my first of several rehabs. I resented being there, I resented all the counselors, and I was sure I was just a victim of circumstance. Surely others my age drank and did drugs the way I did. I was just unlucky; I got caught too easily. People were watching me closer because I was on the honor roll, I thought. I remember being taken to my first meeting while in that rehab and falling asleep. My counselor wasn't amused. One member at the meeting asked me if I thought this was all a joke, as he angrily rolled up his sleeves to show me his track marks, explaining to me that this was a "serious" disease. If I thought it wouldn't happen to me, I was wrong, he added. I laughed! Of course he was wrong! He was an old, broken-down street drunk. I was just an unlucky kid who got caught. I was at the wrong place at the wrong time. I'm not like you! Leave me alone and let me drink. I'll quit if it ever gets that bad.

I don't remember a thing I was told in rehab, but I do remember my best friend's father coming in and telling me his story. Apparently, he had another life before being my friend Tim's father. He had been a drunk and done all sorts of terrible things to his former family. I was blown away. This was one of the nicest guys I'd ever met. I used to think that when I grew up, I'd want to be like Tim's dad. He had been sober for eighteen years through Alcoholics Anonymous. He didn't talk to me a bit about my drinking; he just told his story. I thought that was cool. Then he left.

A few weeks later, a few guys close to my age came to do the same thing: they told their stories and they didn't preach. They said they found sobriety in AA. This was in 1988, and I know where two of those three guys are today. One is still sober. I got out of rehab, thinking I wanted to be sober, but really I just wanted to get the heat off. That took about a month. By then, my parents accepted my drinking but not doing drugs, so I got to know alcohol much better. Soon I was in an outpatient rehab again, this time with drug testing, so my drinking started to take off. Previously, alcohol was something I just did while smoking pot and taking LSD; now it was all about the bottle. I started drinking every night after work, to the point where soon I couldn't sleep without it. One night, when I hadn't had a drink for a couple of days, I found myself lying in bed staring at the ceiling. I had never felt more insanely thirsty in my life. I was willing to steal cars, break into houses, anything to get a drink. I broke into my parents' liquor cabinet and quickly drained a bottle of vodka. I was blacked out before I could walk back to my room. I woke up the next morning in the bathtub with vomit everywhere. I tried to tell my father I had the flu. He just shook his head in disgust. I found out years later that he had watched his own father drink himself to death in Cleveland, in the early days of AA. He knew what I was doing.

By this time, my parents had put locks on their bedroom doors, on the second-story bedroom windows, on their bedroom closet, and on a safe inside the closet. I had been stealing from my parents and beating up my sisters completely without conscience. A typical friendship for me lasted about a month or two, as that was about how long it took people to realize that all I wanted them for was alcohol and drugs. No one would party with me, so I partied alone, getting people to buy booze for me after work, or smoking stolen pot at a vacant lot a block from my house, so I could sleep.

I met Rich in my third rehab. I had been kicked out of private school and was starting at a new public school. Rich was the only one there who honestly wanted sobriety. He was a hippie kid like me, a year younger, and he went to meetings. He invited me, so I went. I knew people got sober in AA, but I didn't think you could get sober at my age. Seeing Rich and meeting other young people was the beginning of hope for me. Rich had 120 days, which to me was incomprehensible. My longest period of sobriety had been maybe twenty days. By then I was always overcome; I had to drink, by any means necessary. I did two meetings a week and began to try everything described in the chapter "More About Alcoholism" to control my drinking. I so badly wanted to drink normally, because I could see that I sure couldn't go more than twenty days before going nuts. Imagine what would happen to me if I gave it up forever!

My last drunk was pretty featureless, but the morning after sure wasn't. At 4:00 A.M. on February 24, 1990, my father came into my room with a heavy-built friend of the family. He told me the family had had enough of my abuse, living in fear of me, watching me drag them down while killing myself. He was sending me to a long-term wilderness boot-camp-style program in Utah, and if that didn't work, he said, I'd be on my own, out

81

on the streets at seventeen. I had no street smarts whatsoever and was not ready for this option. On the plane that morning, I looked at the handcuffs on my hands and gave up. I had never felt so powerless in my life. I couldn't drink successfully, and I couldn't stay sober. I decided that when I returned from boot camp, I would go to AA and do whatever I had to do to stay sober.

Boot camp taught me a little about one day at a time. When I got back, I just kept going. I went to the meetings Rich took me to, and I went to my first young people's meeting, the Young People R Us meeting in Hermosa Beach, California, which still meets today. There I found young people who went to meetings seven nights a week. I followed them around and never had a free night at home for the next year. I got a sponsor, went to meetings, and stayed sober for a year. Life got tolerable sober, but it was far from good. At a year sober, I found myself in torturous pain, crying, "Why do I feel so horrible? I have a year of sobriety! You told me it would get better!"

My friends pointed out a few things: I showed up to every meeting late. I had a sponsor who didn't call me on my defects and who wasn't on me to work the Steps. I had done Steps One, Two, and Three, but I hadn't even approached Step Four.

I got a new sponsor and started Step Four. But outside of going to meetings, putting a dollar in the basket, and not drinking, my life didn't look much different. The way I behaved, my parents were still eager for me to live elsewhere. My mother enrolled me in college at Cal State Long Beach (so much for Harvard), and even got me a job washing dishes there. I stayed sober the next year, but I also slept until noon, skipped classes, sold drugs, lied to my parents to get them to send me money, and treated my dormmates horribly. I burned that bridge completely. And as my parents said I had to pull it together before they would give me another dime for college, I followed the Grateful Dead for the next two years, staying sober, and living in Colorado. I was approaching my sober bottom.

All this time, I went to meetings religiously. I always had a sponsor. I kept working the Fourth Step. But I didn't want to be told what to do.

My freedom in AA, as I understood the Traditions, meant that I could do what I wanted, and no one would tell me differently. By the end of my third year of sobriety, I was a beaten man. I hadn't had a drink, but I had been carrying around an ever-expanding Fourth Step for a year. Insisting that no one would ruin my fun, I scoffed at the "AA Nazis" in my area. However, I was not having fun anymore. I was $2,000 in debt, my sober friends were abandoning me, and I was ready to go back out. I gave up for the second time and began attending a meeting I had always feared – the South Bay Survivors. I asked one of the old-timers to be my sponsor, someone who wouldn't be my friend or trade Dead tapes with me. Larry had me call him every day, show up at my home group an hour early, make the coffee, and come to his house every Sunday to work the Steps. I thought this was a little excessive. After all, I had three years. But I was beaten and willing.

As soon as four months later, I felt like a new person. I read my Fifth Step, started making amends to my family, and began attracting new friends. The Promises, which I had almost given up on, came on like a rush. I started working with a new guy, taking him through the Steps, and getting involved in service. I used to yell at Larry when, in answer to my whining, he would ask me how my next amends was going. I screamed, "You never listen to me!" I saw later that he heard every word, and he knew that the solution was in those amends.

Life today is amazing! In the past six years, I've lived in the remote Utah wilderness with no meetings but with lots of Grapevines, speaker tapes, and meditation. I've worked in Alaska, seen a few more concerts sober, gone to college, and now graduate school. I have a job that I like and where they like me. I have friendships today, some as long as I've been sober. I call my parents and sisters once a week, just to see how they are and they like hearing from me. I wash my dishes, clean my room, make my bed, and pay my bills. I've found that I'm not a cordless model: I need to plug into God in the morning and check in several times a day just to make sure I'm still plugged in. I am active in a Buddhist group, where several of my AA buddies are also members.

I have no idea how I made it this long, or what has kept me sober. But if I were to guess, I'd say that it has something to do with the slogan, "Keep coming back – no matter what." I've stayed active in service, especially at Young People's AA conferences, where I first got a glimmer of hope that I could be sober and have anything in the world if I put AA first. I still go to three meetings a week. I talk to my sponsor several times a week, and I'm lucky enough to work with several new members. I have also attended my Young People's group every Tuesday night for five years. It meant so much to me when the same people showed up every week in the same place when I was new, so I try to do that today, because no matter what else is going on, I can do that. I don't have to say anything spiritual or even be in a good mood. I just have to show up. The group has now grown, from twelve people a week to sixty or seventy solid home group members, plus tons of new people who were just like me when I showed up – eyes wide in wonder at the idea that young people like us can be sober in AA. All I have to do is share my story with them, one drunk to another.

Steve B.
Salt Lake City, Utah
November 2000

Meditation for Hammerheads

I was in Al-Anon when I was introduced to meditation. I had gone to get help with an alcoholic girlfriend who was in AA. I had no idea I was alcoholic, although a long string of alcoholic girlfriends should have been a clue. Al-Anon introduced me to a way of life that included a program of spiritual growth. Still, when one of my group members suggested that I meditate, my response was, "You meditate. I'm going to go beat on the cat." I don't abuse animals; it was just something I said to shut this guy up. I envisioned some bearded guy in flowing robes sitting on a mountaintop in the lotus position. I figured meditation was something only swamis and gurus did. He knew I probably needed to slow down, as my speech was so fast that most people were still processing the first sentence, while I was already on the next paragraph. At that point, my life could have been compared to driving 100 miles per hour toward a concrete abutment. If someone called me hyper, it would have been kind. I was out in the yard raking leaves one day and the answer came – the answer to a question that had been bothering me. I figured it must have come from God, because of the rightness of it and the fact that I hadn't had an original thought in my life. I thought, If God is trying that hard to get through to me, perhaps I could meet him halfway.

Shortly afterward, I noticed one of my coworkers, an older fellow named Fletcher, sitting with his eyes closed at his workstation during lunch. Fletcher was a deeply spiritual person. I sometimes went to him for a pep talk when I was feeling low, and I always came away ready to move heaven and earth. So one day, I rapped him on the shoulder and asked, "Fletch, whatcha doin'?" He said, "I'm meditating." So I asked, "What's that?" He explained that it recharged his batteries, helped him slow down, and organized his thinking a little better. He asked me if I wanted to learn how. I said, "Sure," and he told me just to sit upright, close my eyes, breathe regularly, and think of some spot that made me feel really good – a mountaintop, the beach, the desert, or wherever. Silently reciting a favorite prayer, he said, was also helpful. The object was to shut down the physical senses so that the spiritual senses could open up. And when you wanted to come back, you just thought about coming back. He told me to do it for fifteen or twenty minutes, then if nothing happened, to bag it and call it a day. A quiet location where I wouldn't be disturbed was also a prerequisite. A sudden, loud noise or someone rapping you on the shoulder could have the same effect as a bad acid trip: part of me would still be out there when I came back. Distractions would intrude, he explained, but I could simply think, "I will return to my meditation" and go on. He also said, "Don't be surprised if it takes a little while to get into." He knew I was a hammerhead.

Three weeks went by, and I was doing this meditation thing daily. So I went up to him and said, "Fletch, this is bogus. It ain't happening." He smiled and told me to hang in there a little longer. He said if the only thing that happens is I sit there in the dark with my eyes closed and do nothing for fifteen minutes, I was ahead of the game.

One day I was doing my meditation and thinking how bogus it was. I could hear the cafeteria crew crashing around, the air handler above my head sucking air through the plant ventilation system, and the clock ticking. Then I connected. I was totally enveloped in this warm, pulsing, deep purple wave that advanced and receded with my breath. I was totally aware of my immediate surroundings, yet part of me was somewhere else. I basked in this radiant bliss for about twenty minutes. Then I got back and asked Fletch what the purple was. He looked up and said, "Oh, that's the God force." I asked him what that was, and he said, "You know – love, peace, and healing." I felt calm and refreshed. We talked some more, and I knew I had latched onto something special.

Years later and sober in AA, I was at a flea market one Sunday where one of the vendors had an entire table filled with meditation books. I picked one up and read of cancer cures that are common with intense daily meditation. I realized right then that God had given me everything I needed in the Twelve Steps of Alcoholics Anonymous to live a sober, happy life. I had always been looking to external sources for help. The goal of AA is for me to be healthy, happy, and whole. On the weeks that I meditate regularly, everyone seems to be so nice.

On the weeks when I slack off, old thoughts return that will lead back to old behavior if I don't get back on the beam. Some folks have a favorite meditation spot. I have been able to hook up everywhere I have tried – a doctor's waiting room, a deserted cafeteria, or the cab of my truck. The only time I am not able to connect is when I am so upset that any connection is impossible. The smartest thing for me to do then is to talk to someone who is saner than I am and get my sick, sorry, suffering butt to a meeting. Now fourteen years sober, I realize that meditation is another tool to help my type-A personality to calm down and enjoy the ride.

Bob D.
Springfield, Massachusetts
April 2004

Sk8ting Through Life

It's a perfect summer Saturday afternoon in midtown Sacramento. The yearning to commune with my skateboard and to get back to what used to be everything to me is pulling me to the converted warehouse that is the closest skate sanctuary from my room at the halfway house on 23rd to the end of B Street on the other side of the railroad tracks down by the American River. Absentmindedly, I readjust the chinstrap on my helmet as I skate along, thinking about the tricks I'm going to try.

The early afternoon light flickers in high through the broad leaves overhead and the wind cools the beading sweat on the back of my neck as I near the railroad tracks. The hairs on my arm stand on end as I realize I'm already putting expectations on my session just by imagining what I want to see happen. I really hate that word, expectations. Alcoholics Anonymous — of which I'm a six-month and still-counting member — suggests living without them because expectations screw everything up: relationships, sessions, lives, and even perfect summer afternoons in Sac town.

Hmmm. I don't want to ruin my session before I even get there, so I have to let those expectations go. Have to turn 'em over to the Big Kahuna in the sky. Just need to let it flow, have fun, kick back, and watch, because more will always be revealed.

When I arrive at the end of the roughshod road and step into the cavernous yawn of the old warehouse that is the skate cathedral, I am in awe. A ramp has miraculously appeared since my last visit. Six feet tall, twenty-four feet wide, seven-foot extensions, and steel coping make the ramp a tantalizing temptation. I check my helmet strap and jump on. The motion generates a sound something akin to a giant vacuum cleaner on slow-mo. Vhroomm! Vhrooom! with each pass it goes. Coming off a 50/50, I lose my footing and slam my head against the masonite ramp. Lying on the flat bottom, my head rings as little sparks of light flicker in my peripheral vision like an acid flashback.

I run back up the steep eight-foot transition, drop in, and try again as I shake off the shock of the first slam. I slowly build up speed and then, arming myself with all the self-will I can muster, I drop in, pop off the lip, grab the outside edge of my board, and hold on for dear life. For too long, I hold on. I hold on even though it doesn't feel right. Paying for my willfulness and ignorance of my intuition, I slam hard again. My head is ringing. Stars are flying. My elbows are screaming again in bruised and swollen pain. This is insane, I think while painfully righting myself from the prone position of the slam. I need to step back and reevaluate my approach because my way just isn't working.

My will got me into AA so why should I try and impose it here? Wallowing in self-pity and watching the other skaters enjoy their session, the definition of insanity that is thrown around the rooms of AA comes to mind. They say insanity is doing the same thing over and over again expecting different results. I figure that I need to do something different.

The late afternoon light and the Delta breeze waft serenely over us and through the park. I'm looking down at the mammoth "U" structure before me. A prayer just might release me from the bondage of fear and of self. This notion, as if by providence, pops into my head. Remembering all those foxhole prayers made during my drunken years of debauchery and self-indulgence causes doubts. This prayer has to be different. Asking God to help me land this trick would be just like all those selfish 9-1-1 prayers I had made when I was out there. I sit for a minute enjoying the breeze while thinking about thinking.

What is my part in this whole affair of self-will run riot? How has fear come to run my thoughts? Rather than trying to do the Big Kahuna's will, I'm trying to impose my own, I realize. It has to be his will, not mine. If I can't pray for what I have, I have to pray for the Big K in the sky to remove my fear. Accepting that it is there is the first step to liberation. "Of course! The Serenity Prayer! How could I be so oblivious?" Closing my eyes, I say it out loud. "Oh, Big Kahuna in the sky, grant me the serenity to accept the things I cannot change, the courage to change the things I can, and wisdom to know the difference."

Opening my eyes, I see another skater on the opposite deck of the ramp smiling at me. I smile back.

Breathe, relax, trust the process, I say to myself, envisioning the setup for the air before even dropping into the transitions. I have to place the front foot just behind the front truck bolts, position the back foot to pop the tail off the lip, have a good amount of speed, ready the left hand to grasp the outside edge of my board while in the air for a split second, and then let go. It's the last step, releasing the board in midair, that takes faith. If I do the proper footwork, the aforementioned steps — just as I do in Alcoholics Anonymous with the Twelve Steps of recovery — and have enough velocity, all it would take to pull myself back into the ramp would be the belief, the faith, that it was possible. I have to let go of it completely and trust the process, just as I do in AA.

Instinct and logic tell me to bail out of it when I hit my peak in the air. They scream at me, "You can't just fly through the air like that! What about gravity, huh?" It's counter-intuitive and goes against all logic, that's how I know that it is spiritually the right thing to do. If all I have is a dollar in my pocket and I'm at a meeting, logic tells me to save it for myself for later. If I give it to AA, and have faith in the process, it will come back to me in ways I can't even imagine.

Spirituality is not based on logic, it is faith-driven. Faith makes the impossible possible. Faith has allowed me to be clean and sober for six months. Flying through the air on my skateboard is a test of faith that releases me from the bondage of self, helps me confront my fear, and takes me away from my overly analytical, logical mind.

One more deep breath before I drop in. Vhroomm! Vhroomm! Rolling backward into a tail stall on the opposing wall, I position my feet. Dropping back in, I build speed by crouching low. I'm popping the tail off the lip now, up and over the coping I fly. Grabbing the outside edge of my board, I hit my peak. Now is the moment of truth. I've done all I can at this point. I have to let go and trust in the process: courage instead of fear. Momentarily, I float. Then, the most beautiful sound in the world: all four wheels of my skate touching down on the ramp's smooth surface at the same time. It's a sound of self-assuredness, so satisfying, clean, and true. I'm rolling up the other wall of the ramp now, smiling.

Afterward, the other skater asks me, "Were you praying before you dropped in?"

"Yep. I was," I answer. "It makes me remember why I started skating."

"Cool."

Baxter J.
Sacramento, California
September 2005

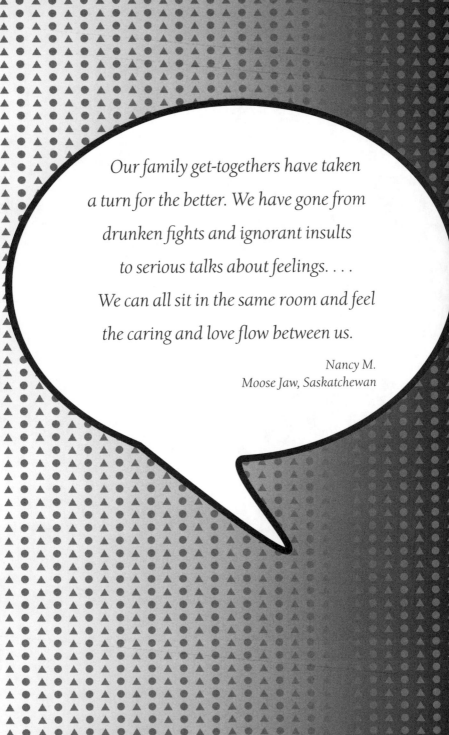

Our family get-togethers have taken a turn for the better. We have gone from drunken fights and ignorant insults to serious talks about feelings. . . . We can all sit in the same room and feel the caring and love flow between us.

Nancy M.
Moose Jaw, Saskatchewan

Section Five: **FAMILY CONNECTIONS**

My Father's AA

Friends of my parents had a pool and they'd throw wild parties. My sisters, the other kids, and I would swim while the parents drank. We knew they were all drunk when the singing started. My mother would get out her accordion and wake up my father, who was usually passed out, and they would do their famous duet of the Titanic song, a cheerful little ditty about disaster. "Husband and wives, little children lost their lives . . ." with everyone joining in on the chorus of, "It was sad . . . ." The song kind of summed up our family life. We were sinking fast.

When I was twelve, I threw a little New Year's party up in my room while my parents had a party in our basement. My buddies and I drank vodka, scotch, and rum I'd smuggled up in baby jars. We were having a great time until I decided I needed more. (The phenomenon of craving had set in, even then.) My father was actually relatively sober that night and he knew instantly that I wasn't. He flew into a rage. "What are our neighbors going to think when their kids come home from our house drunk?" I wanted to tell him the neighbors knew all about us. He was always coming home from work falling-down drunk and I'd have to stop playing with my friends to help him inside.

My father felt that as long as he was making a good living, no one could say anything about his drinking. But when I was fifteen, his company gave him an ultimatum: Quit drinking or be fired. After a month in a rehab he felt he knew all he needed to know and that he would quit drinking on his own. He made it a couple of months. After the second rehab, he got a sponsor and started going to meetings.

The palms of my father's hands used to turn red when he was tense and they were red most of the time in those first months. Sundays were particularly hard; he didn't know what to do with himself. Friends of his from AA would drop by and that seemed to help. They were a strange bunch, often revealing degrading things about themselves and then laughing uproariously about them. And these people wouldn't disappear when there was trouble, like his old drinking pals did. Instead, they came by more often. Sometimes his sponsor and this old guy Walter (who everyone treated with reverence) would come for dinner on Sundays. Walter had been sober since 1942 and told good stories about the early days of AA. Then they'd all head off to the Sunday night meeting at the rehab and I'd head to my room to smoke dope.

For several years, I'd been smoking pot every day, using amphetamines to keep up with school work, and experimenting with LSD. However, it was nothing like my father's drinking. I wasn't trying to get stupefied. I was altering my consciousness. I practiced Transcendental Meditation and read books about Zen. I was on a quest for enlightenment.

The summer before college, I got a job at a nice restaurant where they taught me about fine wines. This was definitely different from my father's drinking: he was a shot-and-a-beer guy, I was a connoisseur. My first weekend at college, I introduced my new dormmates to sophisticated drinking – and promptly threw up all over the hall.

Adopting my father's former attitude, I thought that as long as I performed well in school, no one could hassle me about my drinking. My first semester I was an honor student and won a writing award. By junior year I was on academic probation. The blackouts got more frequent. But this was still not my father's drinking. I was studying writing, and drinking was a necessary part of the creative process. I drank what my favorite writers drank, but it didn't help me write like they wrote.

My father bought me a car so I could visit home on weekends. I racked up parking tickets and expected my father to pay them. The little things he went out of his way to do for me, I took for granted. Only occasionally would I stop and consider that he had completely changed his character.

I remember being in his room one day and seeing the word "Communicate" posted on his mirror. My father? Wanting to communicate?

It started to become clear that I had a drinking problem. One Sunday morning, he got a call from the state police. My car was smashed up on the

95

side of the highway. He ran downstairs to find me passed out in my bed with several cuts on my arms and head. Oh yeah, I'd hit a tree. I talked my way out of trouble with the police and minimized the whole thing. When he actually saw the wrecked car, it took his breath away. It was amazing that I had survived. I heard years later that he'd cried that night at the Sunday night meeting. By then I was already drunk again, and joking about it with my friends.

I told my parents not to come to my college graduation – I was too bohemian to bother with rituals like that. The truth was, I had several incompletes thanks to drinking. I moved in with my parents, telling myself that without the pressure of rent to pay, I could finish up my incompletes, graduate, and get on with my life. After a month I hadn't finished any papers, just lots of bottles. My father invited me to a restaurant for lunch and I steeled myself for the "get a job" speech. Instead, he told me his story. I remember that what sliced right through my denial was when he said that he hadn't gotten into trouble every time he drank, but every time he got into trouble, the bottle was behind it. He offered to send me to the same rehab he had gone to. I was too confused and beleaguered to say no. And I was curious. What if this was my problem? What if I wasn't an awful human being, just one who was sick with alcoholism?

Everyone at the rehab knew my father and was looking out for me. At the daily lectures, I learned about the disease concept, and in group I started to see how grandiose and self-centered I was. I went to the Sunday night meeting that my father had chaired off and on for years and when I moved back with my parents, my father and I went to meetings together. However, it was still "my father's AA," not mine, and I didn't try to make it mine by finding a sponsor or a home group where I fit in. Instead, I tried smoking pot, and days later I was drunk, too drunk to drive. I called home hoping to get my sister to come and pick me up. My father answered. I tried to disguise my voice, but it was clearly me, clearly drunk. He drove me home, not saying a word. Several days before he'd written, "Meeting Makers Make It" on a chalkboard. I ripped it off the wall, then took a swing at him. Fortunately, I was so drunk that I was easily subdued.

I decided to move back to my college town and figure out this drinking thing on my own. My father knew it was a geographic, but he paid for my plane ticket and wished me luck. I had to get obliterated to stop the voice in my head that told me I had no business drinking. As bad as things got, I refused to go back to AA, but I did decide to try counseling. It was a study in half measures and it availed me nothing. I managed to put together three months of not drinking and told my father about it (leaving out the part about smoking pot every day). He sent me a three-month chip taped to the responsibility statement: "I am responsible. When anyone, anywhere reaches out, I want the hand of AA always to be there. And for that: I am responsible." It was his disclaimer: This isn't your father sending you this, it's a fellow AA member. Three months later, I got another chip.

Shortly after this, I learned that my father had liver cancer. I decided it was time to get my act together and forced myself to go to a meeting. Standing awkwardly by the coffee pot, I heard my name. I was sure it was someone from the rehab who'd been sober the last two years while I'd been getting wasted. It turned out to be my creative writing teacher from college. I was shocked to see him there. He wasn't at all surprised to see me. I would never have found the right sponsor, so the right sponsor found me. Here was a guy I couldn't snow with all my literary reasons for needing to drink. Here was a guy I knew was smarter than I, so when he said there was no mental defense against the first drink, I listened. He helped open my closed mind enough so I could at least try to pray.

That year, we all came home for the holidays. My mother sent us a photo beforehand so we wouldn't be shocked when we saw my father. His thick black hair was gone, his face had aged twenty years, and his arms and legs were like twigs. He and I went to meetings every day he felt up to it; we brought along a cushion so he'd feel more comfortable. It was a difficult Christmas. I still get choked up every year when I hear Judy Garland sing those lyrics about being together, "if the fates allow."

A month later I came for another visit. While I'd only been clean for four months, it'd been a year since I'd had a drink. My sponsor told me that if my father wanted to celebrate, then I should do what made him happy. We went to his home group and he presented me with a one-year coin, the very one he'd gotten after his first year. He said it had a good track record.

On the drive home, he asked me to pull over. He opened the door and vomited. I figured he was still getting chemo, that sort of thing happens. Then I saw that he'd vomited blood. I was overwhelmed, but he kept a cool head and soon we were at the emergency room. It was very busy, and I couldn't get them to pay attention to us, but then he threw up more blood, and they quickly took him inside. I didn't know what to do or think so I just repeated the Serenity Prayer over and over. An hour later they told us that they didn't know why, but the bleeding had stopped, and we could come back and see him. He was propped up on a gurney, pale, but smoking a cigarette and smiling.

A day before I left, I asked if I could talk with him. I wasn't up to the Ninth Step yet, but I spoke to him about regretting the things I'd done that had hurt him. He told me not to worry about it – all was forgiven. I wanted to say more, but I got the feeling he couldn't handle any more emotion just then, any more sorrow or regret. Maybe we both could have had a good cry together. As it was, I did my crying staring out the window of the airplane, knowing I would never see him again.

At his memorial service, his AA friends were there, as they'd been for the last eight years. More than any other accomplishments in his life, his service to the Sunday night meeting and the hand he extended to the still-suffering alcoholic defined his life.

In the back of my mind I felt like I deserved to drink again. "Poor me, poor me, pour me a drink." If I'd talked about it to anyone, I might not have acted on it. But I kept quiet, went on a road trip with some work friends, drank again, and blacked out again. The next morning we passed within a mile of where he's buried. I thought to myself, The one thing he wanted for you was that you stay sober. Instead, you used your feelings about him to justify drinking, and within twenty-four hours you were as bad as ever. What is that if not powerless? After one more "convincer" I finally became willing to do whatever it took. I actually did some of the things my sponsor suggested, and started telling him when something was bothering me instead of storing it away for the next time I needed an excuse to drink. I began doing service and worked the Steps.

On my first real anniversary, I dug out the coin he'd given me and said a prayer of thanks. For my next eight anniversaries, my mother would send me another one of his coins, and I'd feel a deep sense of connection with him. I went to the AA Archives in New York and looked at a photo from the 1980 International Convention in New Orleans. He was there, somewhere in the crowd. I've been to the last few and I feel like he's there with me.

Last year, I was helping my mother go through some old boxes and I ran across a cassette tape that said, "Walter's Talk." A chance to hear more of Walter's stories about the early days. I decided to play it on my upcoming anniversary. That night, after a joyous celebration at my home group, I put the tape into a player, relaxed into my favorite chair, and prepared to hear Walter. But the first voice on the tape wasn't Walter's, it was my father's. He was chairing the meeting. As I listened to him recite the Preamble, tears welled up in my eyes. My twelve-year-old came in. "Is that ... your father?" I nodded and he sat down next to me. We listened as my dad told the crowd at the Sunday night meeting they were in for a treat. I felt the hand of AA and the hand of my father reach across the years. It was there for me, just the way he always wanted it to be.

J. W.
Maplewood, New Jersey
March 2005

Lost in the Shadows

In November 1974, in the midst of studying for midterm exams, I walked into my first Alcoholics Anonymous meeting in Westport, Connecticut.

Friends at school had questioned my rather unorthodox drinking habits, and after one too many beers, a close friend asked me to get help. As a favor to her, I said I'd give AA a try. I'd show her I wasn't that bad.

I was nineteen years old and a sophomore at Fairfield University. Even though I was serious about my grades and preparing for my career, the pressure of doing well all the time got to me. No matter how well I did at school, I couldn't help but compare myself to my older brother, the boy genius in my family who had graduated from Harvard Law School and become an attorney.

As youngsters, my four siblings and I tended to get lost in the shadow of my brother's success. No matter what we did, our accomplishments always fell short of our brother's in my father's eyes. But as I grew up, I did have my successes and always rewarded myself for a job well done. When I got an "A," I saluted my hard work with a beer. When I was elected president of the National Honor Society, I patted myself on the back and toasted myself.

I graduated in the top five percent of my high school class and was eager to pursue my undergraduate studies. I met my match in college, however, when I saw that the students were equal to me intellectually. An extra glass of beer at the university's rathskeller took the edge off at the end of each day, and I quickly discovered I preferred that blurry, drunken state to reality. Going through life mocus was looking more and more desirable to me than making good grades and going out into the work world.

I knew that leaving the alcohol alone was getting harder and harder, because it had become my most intimate friend. How would I face the world — and the rest of my young life — without booze? I couldn't imagine it. I called the Fairfield County Intergroup and discovered there was a meeting that night in a church on Main Street in Westport.

I gathered all the courage I could muster and walked into the AA meeting. I'll never forget my first impression of it: several AA members stood around the coffee pot, laughing easily with one another while sharing snippets of their day. Steam rose from the coffee cups they held with steady hands. Snow fell lightly outside the church, a beautiful, old, white building that emanated peace. I saw people sharing and people caring, even though I didn't really understand what was going on that first night.

When the speakers shared, I could relate to their feelings, although my story was very different from theirs. I sat back in my chair and took everything in, awed by the ease with which they poured out their guts. I could relate to their hand-to-hand combat with alcohol, to their resistance to joining a "cult," to their paralyzing fear of reaching out to someone else for help.

I immediately felt at home and accepted for who I was. For the first time in my life, I no longer had to carry the weight of the world on my shoulders. I didn't have to be the best, and I didn't have to be the worst, either. I could fit right in. Mostly, I didn't have to do anything alone anymore.

I had one more drunk after that first meeting. It was on January 1, 1975, and that remains my anniversary date. I was home on Long Island during the holiday vacation, and I couldn't resist the temptation of knocking back a few, getting behind the wheel of my car, and driving around my village. I couldn't stand up straight on my own two feet, but I thought I was competent to drive.

Somehow I got to my parents' home and fell into bed. When I woke up at 4:00 A.M., I walked into the bathroom, sat on the edge of the bathtub, and wondered what had happened. Glancing down at my hands, I wondered why I'd lifted that first drink to my lips.

I cried until I was blue in the face, but I didn't cry over regrets or missed opportunities. I wept from the pain and despair that only an alcoholic knows. I cursed the genes that gave me this disease, and then I asked, "Now what are you going to do about it?"

I had tried quitting on my own and that hadn't worked. I had tried intellectualizing the problem away and that hadn't worked. At that moment, in the stillness of the house, I felt something stir deep inside me. I felt God's hand holding mine and an enormous wave of relief washed over me.

God was with me that cold New York morning as night slipped away and daylight took its place. I asked him to help me not drink just for that day. I asked him to stay by my side and guide me no matter how jittery I felt from the withdrawal of alcohol. I asked him to protect me through my fears, my terror, and my uncertainty. I said out loud that I would open up my heart to him, and a calm came over me that I hadn't felt since making my First Holy Communion as a Catholic many years before. I trusted in God again, and I believed that if I went back to AA and worked the program to the best of my ability, he would carry me through the tough times. And I knew I had a good chance of success, because I knew that I would go to any lengths to stay sober. Once I made up my mind to do something, I did it. I didn't care if others believed it; this time I knew it was true.

Later that morning, I drove back to Westport. I stayed with friends until school resumed and concentrated on making meetings and getting to know people who were serious about sobriety.

I learned how to take things one day at a time, even though I was a busy person who had places to go and people to see. Although I was a teenage alcoholic and sat in rooms with people twice my age, I didn't focus on that because I was too busy listening to their pearls of wisdom.

Eventually, I left Fairfield and finished college at home on Long Island. I got a job in my field and pursued an M.A. at NYU. When I graduated in May 1981, I celebrated with a vengeance, because I'd earned that degree sober, through hard, hard work, and with the help of people in AA.

Time passed. My brother, the Harvard graduate, joined AA four years ago and I celebrated twenty-six years in January. My brother and I have joined hands in the rooms of AA and have found peace. We don't compare our lives and our accomplishments anymore; we just accept each other the way we are. I drank from age thirteen to nineteen, so alcohol robbed me of my adolescence. But I've learned to grow up in AA.

Claire L.
Mineola, New York
March 2001

Ripped Jeans and Threadbare High-Tops

My name is Gina and I'm an alcoholic. Eleven years ago at the age of sixteen, I couldn't say these words. It was October 1986, and I was sitting in my first AA meeting. My dad had been a member for over eighteen years, and my mom was an Al-Anon member. I remember being five years old, running around the kitchen as the coffeepot rumbled and the air filled with cigarette smoke. AA coffee parties were a regular thing as I grew up. I never dreamed that one day I would be drinking coffee as a member of the group.

I took my first drink at age thirteen. This is also the first time I got drunk. Alcohol took away all my problems. It made me smarter, better looking, stronger, and more outgoing. I was (or thought I was) a super-teen until I turned sixteen. I just got released from the drunk tank, had no place to go, lost my job, got kicked out of school, and had no friends to turn to. To top everything off, I was two months pregnant. Some mother I'd be, I thought as I looked at my ripped jeans and threadbare high-tops.

With my head down, I went to my mom and dad. That cold night in October, we went to an AA meeting. I have to be honest when I tell this part: I wish I could say my whole life changed from this day on; it didn't. Living a life of sobriety didn't come easy. Every weekend was a struggle. I'm not proud to admit it, but I did have a slip that lasted three months. I gave birth to a beautiful girl. She helped open my eyes to the destructive lifestyle I was living. I went back to AA in March, 1987 at the age of seventeen.

Today, my eleven-year-old daughter runs around the kitchen during our coffee parties. My husband and I are both AA members. I still have rough days, but I know where to go when these days crop up — our group's clubroom. I believe anyone can be helped if they have an honest desire to stop drinking. I'm living proof.

Gina L.
The Pas, Manitoba
June 1999

Guess Who's Coming to Dinner?

Alcoholics Anonymous came to me in prison. I was twenty-six years old and starting my fourth jail term. AA came when no one else would. My disease had driven away everybody who ever cared for me. My drinking was all that I had left, and that had stopped working.

There were forty-five days between my last two prison sentences. What occurred in those forty-five days were two car wrecks, two DUIs, and three public intoxications. During the last two weeks, I was living in a toolshed in someone's backyard. Then came the crime that, I was sure in my mind, would place me behind bars for the rest of my life.

On the second night of my confinement, I attempted suicide and failed. On the third night, a corrections officer announced that there was an AA meeting. That was July 1, 1985, and the thought of drinking as a solution has not occurred to me since.

Over the course of the next two months, AA came to me two times a week. On one of those nights, one AA member sat and told me his story, giving me instructions on how I too could have the freedom to live sober one day at a time. I believed in AA because AA believed in me. The day I went to court, I was sentenced to fifty years in prison. I was feeling rather hopeless again, and I questioned whether making it that day was possible. Again AA came to me; it didn't give me sympathy, shame, pity, or guilt. It just gave me the truth: "Jake, didn't you tell us that you were willing to go to any lengths for victory over alcohol? This is it!"

I stayed in jail another thirty days before going off to prison. When I left, my AA sponsor gave me his address and encouraged me to write. He also gave me a book called *Alcoholics Anonymous,* which I still carry. I was told to get involved in the AA group in prison. I had stayed drunk in prison for years before, so I knew it was going to be a rough ride. We had one meeting on Monday nights. At first, the meetings didn't feel that beneficial. I wrote my sponsor a lot of letters, and he wrote back.

Gradually, the meetings got better, and I started a second weekly meeting. Late in 1986, I became involved in AA's service structure and was elected to be my group's GSR. On January 3, 1987, I attended my first area assembly meeting. I showed up in ten pounds of chains and with two armed guards, and AA welcomed me. During the next five years, I didn't miss many assemblies. In 1998, I received a letter from the state telling me that my time had been cut in half. No legal work was being done on my behalf to my knowledge.

My job in prison as an inmate peer-counselor for the drug and alcohol treatment program sent me back to the county jail to start a treatment program at the county level. So I was back in my hometown where it all had started five years earlier. Drunks came and got me, and we went to meetings. I got to see that the meetings on the inside were just as real as the ones on the outside. My sponsor took me to conventions, and I got to stay the whole weekend. Some of my family relations were beginning to be restored. Then, on August 24, 1992, I was released on an early release act, which first-time offenders don't even make.

Two weeks after my release, at a district meeting, I was elected to DCM service, an important part of my recovery. It was an honor to serve AA. My parole situation was strict, to say the least, and rightly so; after all, I'd been released fifteen years early. My movement within the district was limited. When I couldn't get a pass to go to the second assembly meeting of my term, I got angry and resigned my office. It was for the good of my district, I claimed. In truth, Jake didn't get his way: so I showed them.

Over the next four years, I stayed close to meetings, but away from service. I was becoming aware of the things of the world, things I hadn't learned about drunk, like working, paying bills, acquiring stuff, and getting involved in relationships. During this time, I got married, and as the marriage ended, I drifted away from meetings.

Running on self-will, I had tried to fill my life with outside stuff. I bought a house and filled it with things, but I felt empty inside. I was only going to two or three meetings a year now, and before long I got to the jumping-off place again. I tried to die, and failed again. But I didn't drink.

The morning after that suicide attempt I screamed in pain to God, "Okay, God, I give you thirty days to show me that my life is worth living." I went to the noon meeting that day, and a newcomer picked up a thirty-day chip. He was living in a drinking environment, so after the meeting I invited him to move into my home. What I had heard was, "We throw ourselves the harder into helping others." When the newcomer moved in, I thought that God was showing me real quick that my life was worth living.

I was giving service to the Fellowship; I really had something that could be useful to another human being. With the newcomer in my home, I knew that I had to be an example of what to do, so I started going to three or four meetings a week. I also shared my experience on how to work the Steps.

One day he was having trouble on the job, and I said, "Have you ever read about the 'actor who wants to run the whole show?'" I started reading that part of "How It Works" to the newcomer, and about halfway through I became overwhelmed with guilt and started crying. I saw that I had been the actor for four sober years!

My sponsor had moved out west, and I needed help. The next day at a noon meeting, I got a new guide and started putting this program back into my life. An inventory was a good place to start, but of course the easier, softer way was blaming others, such as my ex-wife and my father.

Back in 1985, when my sponsor was taking me through the Steps, I was aware of my deep-seated resentment against my father. I didn't want to even look at it, let alone let go of it back then. My sponsor had told me that in time God would put it in my heart to deal with it, as long as I kept an open mind. My father was still coming up on my resentment list, but my will said that it still wasn't time to deal with it.

Anything would have been perceived as an improvement in my life prior to the newcomer coming into my home. The improvement was that meetings were a part of my life again, I had a new sponsor, and I was working with a drunk. About three months later, I was asked to speak at a meeting in a town forty miles from my home. At the meeting was a woman I had been involved with in 1994. We visited after the meeting, started talking on the phone, and then began dating. Over the years, I had thought of her often, for we had a lot in common. We went to meetings together, and life was good. Anger, however, was still all around me, at work mainly, but the day came when I projected that anger into our relationship and destroyed it.

Looking back, I see that my attitudes and behavior were stripping my soul. The last remnant was lost when my relationship with this woman ended. I worked on my inventory and had long talks with my sponsor, yet I still failed to understand the exact nature of my wrongs. The day that my fit of anger broke up the relationship, I went straight to a noon meeting.

I just sat in a corner in a state of nonparticipation. At the end, we stood and joined hands to say the Lord's Prayer. As the words, "Our Father" were being said, I thought, "Yeah, father will beat your mom and leave you cold and hungry." At that point I knew that it was all over. I had failed AA, because now I hated God. I decided that I would just resign from AA.

Eight days later, the woman I had been in the relationship with called. I could only respond in resentment and hopelessness. She listened for a while and then started reading to me from the "Twelve and Twelve."

At first, I took offense; after all, I knew the words. Then I began to listen, not to the words, but to the emotion in her voice. I heard her concern, compassion, and love. I remembered that I, too, had once shared in that fire of hope that burned through the pain and despair, and pulled me from the pit of total and complete defeat. Could I rise again? Was there still hope? I picked up my inventory and wrote some more. I prayed and cried for guidance. The resentment toward my father had been with me for thirty-eight years. I saw that this resentment had bled into every fiber of my being. My will was turned over all right, turned over to my father and hate. I saw that this resentment must be mastered, but how?

In 1992, newly released from prison, I had had support from my family that I had never dreamed possible. I began to see that I was the only member of the family who still projected anger toward my father. Both my sisters visited him regularly, and my mother invited him to holiday dinners from time to time. Not me, though. I'd stayed away. In 1997, when I was at my mom's for Thanksgiving dinner, the phone rang and I answered it. My father was on the line. I didn't respond to his greeting, but instead handed the phone to my sister. When she got off the phone, she announced that my father was on his way to join us for Thanksgiving dinner. I responded by saying "I hope you have a good time," and then walked out the door. I went to a fast-food place and then to a movie. Sure showed them, didn't I? Now, freshly armed with my new inventory and a desire to be on fire with the program again, I ran to the noon meeting. I put pride and ego in my back pocket and said, "I'm sixteen years sober, and I'm going crazy. I hate my father and resentment is completely destroying my life. Can you please help me?" "Of course," I was told. "You're in the right place." The topic for that meeting became resentment. AAs shared their deep-seated angers, and the pain of growing from them. The resentment exercise in the story, "Freedom From Bondage" was read to me.

At my sponsor's house after the meeting, we talked some more. I really wanted to deal with this thing once and for all. I asked, "How can I be willing to ask God that all of what I want for myself be given to Dad?" My sponsor answered, "Who's asking you to?" "The 'Freedom From Bondage' lady," I said. "That's her experience, Jake. Let's find yours," was his answer. At that point, I remembered a gem of wisdom that I had once heard at a meeting. It goes like this: "There are many paths up the mountain. The view from the top is the same." My sponsor then reminded me that there's another exercise in the Big Book about resentment. It's the Third Step prayer: "Relieve me of the bondage of self." Suddenly, it all became so clear. I had never looked at my anger toward my father without him in it. I had never looked just at myself. At that moment, I had an immediate and overwhelming feeling of the presence of God in my being.

At home I read and prayed for hours. I sat and listened for direction. I realized that I could have, at any point through all of this, made the decision to let go. But it takes what it takes, even in sobriety. Pain is the best messenger that God has. The decision that must be made is to seek God's will through the hurt. The process of self-will in pain is to attack, to re-live the hurt, and to keep defending oneself from hurting again. What happens is, we get so wrapped up in the anger that we forget the joyful person, place, or thing that was torn from us by the hurt. In turn, we never seek or know again the meaningful things that were lost through pain. In the war of self *versus* pain, pain always wins. If I could keep my heart full of wonder at the daily miracles of life in recovery, my pain would not seem less wondrous than my joy.

Well, the messenger of pain had been knocking on my door for a long time, and the day finally came when I took the action to open that door. It had become clear that I had to confront my father. Right, wrong, good, or bad, something had to be done, because what I had been doing for thirty-eight years hadn't worked and never would. I jumped on my motorcycle and rode the 110 miles south to my father's door. I didn't know what I was going to say or do, I just needed to go. What I wanted to tell him was the truth. I wanted to tell him about the unhappiness, about how I had blamed and hated him for years.

At his door, the Third Step prayer came to me again, and I couldn't say anything. God allowed me to see my father without myself in the picture. I saw him for who and what he was, a beaten and broken old man, totally and utterly alone. Now, this wasn't that moment in the Johnny Cash song where "I called him my pa." I still didn't like his actions. But I didn't like my actions, either. I just didn't have to hate anymore. I was free. He, too, was a sick man, and I didn't feel different or alike; I was just there, at peace.

That was October 27, 2001. Returning home, I felt warmth come over me. I was at one with all there is and I thanked God for letting me know him better. When I share this experience at meetings, I'm amazed at the number of members who hold such feelings. I continue to share it in the hope that others may find the freedom I have.

One final note: this was my year to host Thanksgiving dinner for my family. Guess who came to dinner?

Jake W.
Rogers, Arkansas
September 2002

A Family Nightmare

Beause I grew up in an alcoholic home, no one had to educate me about the disease. I had seen it all in my own family, especially in my mother, who was a chronic alcoholic by her late thirties. The atmosphere at home was a sad picture, bereft of emotional support and stability. It was a roller coaster from hell that never seemed to end, or even slow down.

My brother, six years my senior, bailed out when he was sixteen and began his own alcoholic career away from home. He joined the service and went far away. He was the hero I hardly knew. I dreamed he would come back home and take me away from my terrible life. I swore to myself time and time again that I would never drink. I hated alcohol.

But when I was fifteen, I had an opportunity to try it out. It happened on a remote ranch near my hometown. I went with a friend whose family was the band providing the weekend entertainment. We were all camped there and, as I drank, I clearly remember thinking, Well, if you can't beat 'em, may as well join 'em! I drank whiskey to a blackout, but remember that first feeling that said, Finally, everything feels right.

After that weekend, I was like a thoroughbred racehorse at the starting gate, high-strung and ready to hit the ground running — running into alcohol every chance I had. I ran from the past, present, and future; I ran from myself for breaking my vow not to drink.

I soon met a guy just like me, and he was running too, from a family just like mine. At just seventeen, we ran away together. We dreamed our lives would be different, even as we drank together.

When I became pregnant with our daughter, we decided to get married. I slowed way down, sometimes not drinking at all for several months. He continued drinking, which became hard for me to endure sober.

My mom had tried AA and, even though I didn't know much about it, I talked my husband into trying it and went with him. The meeting was in a volunteer firehouse in remote northwestern New Mexico, and it was an open meeting. Of course, I came as the Al-Anon because I could quit drinking and certainly couldn't be an alcoholic. That night became the beginning of my soapbox career, preaching self-righteously to him and others: if only they would quit drinking and get their lives in order, I would be just fine.

We quickly spiraled into the same alcoholic patterns of our families. My baby daughter and I moved back to Dad's for a while (my parents had divorced after I left). He had mysteriously stopped drinking on his own.

During this same period, my brother and his new family moved back to our hometown, too. He drank heavily and was having problems, so my sister-in-law and I attended Al-Anon together. I didn't stay, though, because I had gotten rid of my alcoholic. She kept attending and they stayed together.

Then I met "Prince Charming." He came from a normal home and I let him rescue me from my painful life. We drank socially and had fun. We moved to a bigger city together, drank in the evenings, and enjoyed drinking on weekends. I married my prince a few months later and he legally adopted my little princess. I knew we would live happily ever after.

Back home, my brother had a brush with the law while drinking, went to jail, and then entered a treatment center. He started attending AA on the inside and continued after he came home.

Some time later, he called to ask me about having our mother committed to the state hospital. She was in the last stages of chronic alcoholism and had been on the merry-go-around of hospitals, psych wards, treatment centers, and jail. She had been in and out of AA and had fallen off again and again. I couldn't agree to have her committed, so I silently said my good-byes and thought I'd never see her again. I waited for that final phone call.

Instead, fifteen days before my second little princess was born, my mom got into AA, stayed, and got sober. I doubted it would last and watched cautiously from my city four hours away. She had remarried and my step-dad got sober too!

Then a dark shadow appeared in my fairy tale life. I began drinking socially when my baby was a little older. I picked up right where I left off, drinking nights and weekends.

But the party circle changed. There were roughshod strangers and people I had never seen. My husband developed a drug problem and my world came crashing down again.

Once, right after a party, lit up and self-righteous, I held my husband hostage in our home with one of his loaded guns while our daughters slept in the next room. I ordered him to get help and get straightened up! I wanted our wonderful life back and reminded him again and again that if he would get help, I wouldn't be this way.

He slipped away at daylight (I think I passed out). When I woke up the next morning, I knew paradise was long gone. I was bankrupt spiritually, mentally, and emotionally, and suicidal in a house full of guns. I called my husband at work, but he wouldn't come to the phone (duh!).

A coworker I barely knew asked if I was okay. I said no; he came over and took all the guns away. My husband never came back.

I stopped drinking again and heroically took my soapbox back, blaming my insanity on these alcoholics and addicts around me. A few months later, I reluctantly moved back home, this time with my mom and step-dad.

They became loving parents and grandparents. Both started caring for their own now elderly and frail parents. I stayed away from old stomping grounds and started seeing a guy in AA, a friend of my mom's. Adult Children of Alcoholics had just started and I started going to their meetings. I still lived in fear of a drink and had only one miserable beer that summer with an old friend from high school. Then I decided to go to AA, just to see why I loved alcoholics so much. I attended meetings and still felt unique.

One day in a meeting, a woman talked about the insanity of having held her ex-husband hostage at gunpoint. It was the same nightmare I'd lived. She talked about her periodic alcoholic binges. She called herself a "periodic alcoholic." I had never heard the term. She also described the same shame and remorse I had secretly hidden under my self-righteousness. She and her husband took me under their wings. I would later pick up my one-year chip at a meeting they started.

During my first thirty days, I was hospitalized and nearly died from a ruptured appendix. My new, sober family rallied around me, especially my mother. It took a long time to get better, and she cared for my girls the whole time. About a year later, I fell in love with yet another alcoholic, but this one was sober, and still is. We've been married over sixteen years now, and my brother is his first sponsor. They are not only close in AA, but brothers-in-law, too.

Last year, a longtime dream came true for my husband and me. We traveled from south-central New Mexico to Washington State. We stopped in northwest Montana to visit an AA friend and attended a meeting in her home group.

We went on to my brother's home in Washington. It was his twenty-first AA anniversary, and he requested that his men's stag meeting open up to let his sister attend. When he received his twenty-first year medallion that night, there wasn't a dry eye in that room full of men and me.

Our family has gone from years of one hopeless alcoholic disaster after another to years of collective sobriety and happiness. Real life is still happening for all of us, but we've stayed sober through accidents, illness, and death. We've cried together, laughed together, and prayed for each other. My mom and I have laughed about the "periodic alcoholic" being the stage just before the "chronic alcoholic."

We are grateful. Grateful to be alive, sane, and sober. And grateful to AA that we are a family restored.

Laurie R.
Mayhill, New Mexico
April 2006

Family Connections

I was raised in a good Catholic family with five brothers and sisters. My parents worked hard to support us and make sure we had everything material that we needed. For the most part it was a happy family. All of my

113

older brothers and sisters succeeded in school and went on to college. I was the exception. From an early age, I began getting into trouble. Eventually, I dropped out of high school and took a job working for the carnival.

Just about three years ago, I found the program of Alcoholics Anonymous. My life has improved in immeasurable ways since then. Working through and living the Twelve Steps has helped me to learn how to live a better life.

One thing that is a source of pain and fear in my life today is attending family functions and being reminded of all the years that I brought shame to my family. My eighty-three-year-old grandmother died in a car accident not too long ago, and this was a particularly hard occasion for me to deal with. The last time we talked was a few months before the accident. She asked me about my drinking and if I was still "on the wagon." She also mentioned that my grandfather's brother Art had been an alcoholic and she thought he used to go to "those meetings." That was the last conversation I ever had with her.

While at the funeral home for calling hours, I felt lonely and sad. Here I was, standing alone in the back room of the funeral home, trying not to get in the way of the dozens of people there. I noticed a well-dressed man sitting alone near some of my cousins. I cannot explain why I approached this man and started talking to him. I introduced myself and he told me that he was the son of my great-uncle Art. I told him about my last conversation with my grandmother and that I was coming up on three years' sobriety. He congratulated me, then told me that he had fifteen years himself.

My new friend and I spent the next two days talking, grieving, and sharing experience, strength, and hope. He told me of other members of my family, some of whom were in our program, and how I was not alone. He helped me to understand that my aunts and uncles do not care about what happened in the past and think only of what I am doing for myself today.

Greg A.
Canton, New York
March 2005

Mother, Father, Daughter

Mother

I remember sitting in the bathroom of our worn-down house and watching my mother do her hair and put on her makeup, thinking she was the most beautiful woman I had ever seen. She had an elegance about her that didn't belong in this place. After all the finishing touches, we'd head into town in the back of a taxi and from there only God knew where we'd end up. But it always ended the same way, in some bar in town, mom drunk and the bartender calling my dad to come pick us up.

After twenty years of her drunken insanity, when she was in the worst DTs yet, she was admitted to the first rehab in a series of many. And, after countless prayers and tears, in 1991 she finally caught hold of the Promises of AA, just in time for me to begin a drinking spree of my own. I had been using prescribed narcotics for about four years before that and had long since given up hope that anything would ever change. But change it did, and as I set out to enjoy my newfound nightlife, she began to grow mentally, physically, and spiritually stronger.

As my drinking progressed to out-of-control, she would say things like "I'm praying for you, hon" and "Do you think you've had enough yet?" and (my favorite), "When the pain outweighs the pleasure, you'll try something different."

On August 27, 1999, that day finally came – I had had enough. I went to her house, where she nursed me through my last hangover and took me to my first AA meeting.

There's not much I remember of that meeting except the relief I felt that these people truly understood. At the end of the meeting, when they asked if anyone wanted to join this way of life, I picked up a white chip and sat back down beside my mother. She patted me on the knee and said, "Welcome home, hon. I've been waiting for you."

Father

He was a quiet man as I recall, tall, strong, hard-working, and an alcoholic of the worst type. I have very few memories of tender moments or moments of fatherly concern or even moments of correction or direction. I don't recall ever hearing him say, "I love you."

My younger sister was born in 1967, when I was ten. At that point in my father's life, he'd decided the drink had already robbed him of too much and put the bottle down, cold turkey. I was terrified of him as a drunk and didn't much care for him this way, either. His bursts of drunken anger turned into ten years of silent solitude, looking after my sister, working long hours, and living in what I now know as a state of "dry drunk."

He was introduced, against his will, to the rooms of AA when my mother made her first attempt at sobriety in 1977. However, it was my father who grabbed hold of the program like a man grabbing for the last life vest on a sinking ship, and I liked him even less.

For the next ten years, all I would know of him was that every drunk in town was some kind of insane vision of hope. He even named a stray dog he fed after one of them. He said this dog was like a drunk he knew named Herb who only came in to sleep under the porch when he was worn out and ready to die from fighting. I didn't have a clue what he was talking about.

My father died sober on June 9, 1991. I picked up the bottle one month later.

Beaten and battered like that old dog Herb, I found my way to my first AA meeting on August 27, 1999. I grabbed hold of the program just like a man grabbing for the last life vest on a sinking ship.

By the grace of God and through the rooms of AA, ten years after his death, I began to know my father. Having worked the Twelve Steps to save my own life, I can now look back and know almost exactly when he worked his. I remember his relief when he found out he was not alone; I remember his first sponsor and when he did his Fourth and Fifth Steps; I know now that those Monday-night dinners at my place were when he was doing his

Ninth Step and I know, because of the multitude of AAs at his funeral, that he lived the Twelve Steps of AA every day of his life.

I haven't seen him physically in over thirteen years, but I hear him every day through the AA Fellowship. Because AA is teaching me what true love is, I can hear my father, through the Fellowship, tell me often that he loves me, and I know that I am not alone.

Daughter

"When anyone, anywhere, reaches out for help, I want the hand of AA always to be there. And for that: I am responsible."

My first year of sobriety was a whirlwind, to say the least. The only place I felt safe was at an AA meeting. I went to at least one and often two or three meetings a day, which kept me away from home a lot. But eventually I became more comfortable in my own skin and slowed down enough to realize that my eighteen-year-old daughter was well into her own disease.

How could this have happened? I grew up with alcoholic parents, became an alcoholic myself, and now my daughter? Was there no end to this nightmare?

My mother showed me the perfect example of AA love in my life. She had ten years of sobriety through AA and I knew she hadn't given up on me, so I followed her example. I began to talk very openly and honestly about my own disease, and I stayed as close to my daughter in the darkness of her disease as I safely could. I found ways and reasons to include her in my AA program, like taking her to open meetings at my home group and AA beach cookouts. I even asked her to present my medallion one year.

She became surrounded by my AA Fellowship as I worked my program to save my own life. She began to want to stop, not for herself, but for me. She made a stab at rehab several times. Once I even had her committed, and every night, without fail for three years, I cried and laid my heart out to God to save my daughter and give her a desire of her own to quit.

Then, on September 5, 2003, she found her own spark of hope. She now goes to AA meetings, works the Twelve Steps, and is finding a new way of life. Her spiritual growth teaches me something new every day.

I sat beside my daughter, with her grandmother next to her, and watched her pick up her six-month chip. I could not find the words to describe what AA has done for my family. I had only tears of the deepest gratitude and an immense understanding of the phrase "we would go to any lengths for victory over alcohol."

Penny D.
March 2005

One Thing Leads to Another

I have three brothers and four sisters. We grew up in Moose Jaw, Saskatchewan, and came from a home where mental and physical abuse ran rampant. My father was an alcoholic and my mother was the perfect co-alcoholic. My father left home when I was ten years old, and we had little or no money to live on. If we behaved badly it was common for us to go to bed without supper, plus get whatever beating Mom saw fit to give us. Most of us were accomplished thieves by the time we were twelve or thirteen years old.

Standing back to back with one of my brothers or sisters was a way of life — taking on the world, daring it to take its best shot at us. We all had major trouble in school. We couldn't get along with anyone.

Not surprisingly, most of us turned to alcohol, and in a relatively short time, we were full-fledged alcoholics.

Then, eight years ago, my older sister Jane found this program. For the first two and a half years of her sobriety, she tried to cram it down our throats. Needless to say she didn't get too far. Then all of a sudden she quit trying to make us sober up and started working on herself. After three months she looked so good that my older brother Russ sobered up. Then three months later, Jane's husband sobered up. Two weeks later, I sobered up. Two years after that my older brother Gordon sobered up. On my fourth-year anniversary, my older sister Lois sobered up. Four months later my older sister Cindy sobered up, and my little sister Stella found her way home to Al-Anon.

The alcoholic parent has passed away and the co-alcoholic still chooses to be sick. But our family get-togethers have taken a turn for the better. We have gone from drunken fights and ignorant insults to serious talks about feelings. Spontaneous AA meetings spring up in corners of living rooms and kitchens. We've walked each other through the past, supported each other, helped each other stop playing deadly head games, and made amends for things done. We can all sit in the same room and feel the caring and love flow between us.

When we were drinking, we had the kind of loyalty where we would have died for each other. We did everything we could to protect each other from reality. Now we help each other face reality and deal with it. We can talk about our mother, and face her with the ability to wish her well.

We're no longer fighting back to back but walking side by side. One of the biggest thrills of my life is to watch a newcomer grow in the program, but to see a family member grow is that much more special. To sit in a meeting where there are six of us from the same family is an honor and a privilege.

Miracles happen. Through the grace of God and AA, they will continue to happen for all of us.

Nancy M.
Moose Jaw, Saskatchewan
January 1995

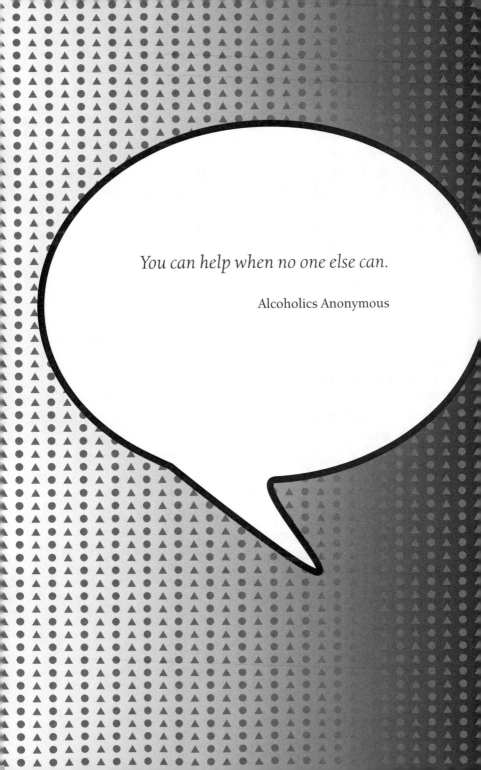

You can help when no one else can.

Alcoholics Anonymous

Section Six: **FRIENDS WE HAVEN'T MET YET:** *Working and Playing with Others*

Death, Interrupted

"My name is Chris, and I'm an alcoholic." This was the first thing I learned how to say when I came here. Believing it, however, was an entirely different story.

I first came to AA at the age of nineteen, which is not unusual by today's standards. I chose to believe that it was, however, especially when so many people said how good it was to see the young people. Here was something that my alcoholic ego could delight in: the spotlight of terminal uniqueness. I basked in that rich glow, proud of the fact that I was my group's youngest member at the time. I had a good sponsor, I got active with my group, I did all the right things on the outside. But inside, I was never quite sure that I really fit in here. I was too young. I hadn't been through enough.

Many, many times I'd heard recited from the podium the prices other alcoholics had paid to be here: broken marriages, car accidents, lost homes, prison sentences. None of these had happened to me. Even the stories of other young people in AA seemed to be worse than mine. I was told to identify and not compare. I learned to put the word "yet" into my speech. I knew that my drinking even then was "no mere habit," so I stayed here, but I didn't identify with most of the experience shared at meetings. I spent a number of years in AA trying to make my own story sound tougher and longer and as violent as I could without actually lying.

Two and a half years ago I became active in carrying the message behind the walls at a women's prison. I found even less identification there, but it kept me grateful that the doors were closing behind me, and not on me. Currently, I serve as the outside sponsor for this facility. Sadly enough, it isn't uncommon for the outside AAs to fail to appear. We've taken to occasionally having our own speaker meetings in the case of such an event, one inmate chairing and three others telling their stories. These meetings are incredibly powerful and moving experiences (the kind that really keep you hooked on prison work).

On one recent Thursday night, it was my privilege to be at such a meeting. A young woman spoke, revealing a story that, as usual, was fifty million times worse than mine. Happily enough for me, however, God caused my ears to hear her story a little differently that night. The first part of her story could have been my own. What I heard was that hers continued.

There is a well-loved AA speaker who visits this area from time to time, and she tells of our deaths having been interrupted by the priceless gift of sobriety, alcoholism being a progressive, fatal disease. God allowed me to realize that night that my sobriety is only an interruption in the rest of that story that could well be my own.

So I no longer begrudge my young age at the time I got sober. I no longer need to creatively embellish my story to feel like I fit in here. Now I joyously celebrate the fact that God has given me nearly eight years in this program.

Chris B.
Norwood, Massachusetts
April 1996

From *Sobriety Rocks!*, March 1998

If there is a presiding spirit of the International Conference of Young People in AA (ICYPAA, affectionately known as "icky-pa"), it might be found in these words from chapter nine of the Big Book: ". . . we aren't a glum lot. If newcomers could see no joy or fun in our existence, they wouldn't want it. We absolutely insist on enjoying life." ICYPAA is the manifestation of that insistence. It proves that nobody's too young for AA and that a sober life can be enjoyed at any age. In the words of one participant: "Sobriety rocks!"

The Young-Timer

I have often heard AA members say, "Young people are the future of AA," and I heard it again recently. I'd like to share my experiences with being the future of AA.

As an adolescent in Alcoholics Anonymous (I sobered up in Ann Arbor, Michigan, three weeks before my fourteenth birthday), I was sometimes mistaken for the child of an AA member. I guess people in AA couldn't really figure out what to do with me, so mostly I was left alone. When I did manage to catch a conversation after a meeting, I got a lot of "You're so lucky!" and "Young people are the future of AA." I didn't feel so lucky, but I quite liked the idea of being the future of AA. I sat in meetings and secretly calculated my future sobriety ("When I'm sixty-four, I'll be fifty years sober."), imagining myself as a beloved old-timer. Eventually I did the math to find that in the year 2000, I would be twenty-eight years old and fourteen years sober – half my life. That seemed cool, and I fantasized about how well-liked I would be, how accomplished and accepted.

It seemed completely normal then to think of myself as a kind of potential person, who could, if I stayed sober, be a real AA member. When you're a kid, some adult or another is always talking to you about your future or your potential. It's the big leverage adults have on you, the justification for everything. "You have so much potential." "You have to think of your future." Having drunk for less than two years, I had some trouble identifying the patterns of my alcoholism. Even though I felt comfortable in AA meetings, I didn't necessarily think I belonged there. I sort of figured that I would fit in better as I got older. I considered taking the advice given to me by well-meaning AAs when I expressed doubt about my condition: to continue to drink until I was completely convinced. But rather than drink again, I latched onto the idea of the "scarcely more than potential alcoholic" described in Step One in the "Twelve and Twelve." This phrase convinced me that AA or Bill or Bob – or someone – understood that kids like me would show up in AA, and this recognition gave me permission to stay.

In 1991 or so, someone from my home group said, "Darren, people like you will lead AA into the new millennium." It was thrilling to hear, for what I heard was, "Darren, you will lead AA into the new millennium." I developed vague fantasies of my future leadership and respectability. Thinking it might make me a leader, I became the GSR of a young people's group and attended an area assembly or two, finding the crowd way too old. I got interested in young people's AA, attending a few International Conventions of Young People in AA and as many young people's meetings as I could find.

In my fourth and fifth years of sobriety, most kids I was sober with in high school got drunk or simply left AA. By my eighth or ninth year sober, I was considered a phenomenon back in my home town – "the one who made it." There were nights I found myself at meetings where I was the youngest person in the room and the longest sober. It is a lonely and frightening experience to feel like you're still too young to be considered a "real alcoholic" and yet sober longer than the other AAs are. I now know I share this experience with others blessed like me.

Ultimately, being sober longer than my age peers and being so much younger than my sober peers unsettled me. I felt pressure in young people's meetings to say the right things, sound a certain way, or represent something to the other kids. It was too much for me. I didn't want the responsibility my sobriety had given me. At the same time, in regular meetings I felt pressure to represent and even defend young people from the older crowd. I felt squeezed by both sides. By year ten, I was rotating my meeting schedule so that I wasn't consistently present at any one group for people to know me or know how long I was sober.

As a teenager in AA, the future was a vast unknown expectation. In my twenties, it became a terrifying pressure. As the years headed toward the year 2000, it became pretty clear that I was not going to lead AA into the new millennium. My fourteenth anniversary and my twenty-eighth birthday came and went in October, 2000. Not surprisingly, nobody asked me to lead anything.

Sober half my life, leader of nothing, I found that I didn't have much of an imagination about what I should do with myself. I took the opportunity to reinvest in AA, getting a new home group and taking the Twelve Steps again thoroughly. Since then, much of the pressure I was feeling has lifted. Part of me knows that I have succeeded simply by staying sober. But I also know that I have failed. Maybe I failed an unreasonable expectation placed on me accidentally by well-intentioned alcoholics. But I then naively took it on myself. That I did so was to my own detriment. I got myself twisted up unnecessarily and probably missed out on opportunities to help other young alcoholics and to be helped by them. Certainly I could have avoided the fear of the too young old-timer if I'd had more contact with the leadership available in Alcoholics Anonymous.

Why people still refer to young people as the future of Alcoholics Anonymous is a mystery to me. All of our newcomers are the future of Alcoholics Anonymous. Young or old, whoever stays sober is the future of AA.

Today I am thirty-one years old, seventeen years sober, chair of my home group, alternate district committee member of my district, brilliantly sponsored, and more or less at peace. But I found myself bristling when I heard that old sentence "Young people are the future of AA" a few weeks ago. I know that it was said in the spirit of AA love and service, but my experience shows that this kind of talk can have a rather "intoxicating" effect on a young alcoholic.

Darren F.
New York, New York
February 2005

From *Sobriety Rocks!,* March 1998

The first ICYPAA was held in April 1958 at Niagara Falls, New York. The press release for the event read, "Youngsters in AA to Meet," and went on to say, "The theme of the conference can be summed up in the apparently paradoxical phrase 'Youth Finds Serenity,'" mentioning the special problems of getting sober for those "under forty." Indeed, from a photo of one of the conference sessions, it looks as if many of those who attended were on the shady not the sunny side of forty. The photo, taken from the back of the room, shows grey and balding pates on the men and women with suits and pillbox hats. The whole affair looks rather stuffy – a far cry from ICYPAA today. The permanent ICYPAA Advisory Council was formed in 1960, at the Milwaukee conference. In the Council's words, it was "established for the preservation of experience and material. . . . Being cognizant that not all young people find our conference or meeting necessary, we do not propose to be a universal answer or a governing body for young people. We believe it beneficial to share our experience with all who request our help, for it is through our sharing that we have learned to function within the framework of the AA Traditions."

A New Generation of Old-Timers

Concern about alcoholism in young people existed in the very beginning of Alcoholics Anonymous and has continued to the present day. The Big Book, published in 1939, refers to young people when it states, "Several of our crowd, men of thirty or less, had been drinking only a few years, but they found themselves as helpless as those who had been drinking twenty years." So Twelfth Step work with young people was occurring in the 1930s. In an article entitled "Bridging the Age Gap" in the July 1950 Grapevine, the author states, "In the last three or four years, groups whose specific aim is to reach the younger alcoholic have mushroomed throughout the country," giving us a glimpse of AA's interest in young people in the 1940s. In the 1950s, young people were sufficiently organized to address their own concerns, and the First International Conference of Young People in AA was held in 1958 in Niagara Falls, New York.

AA's "young people's department," as Bill W. called it in *Alcoholics Anonymous Comes of Age*, actually started in July 1935 with the sobering up of a thirty-year-old man who became AA number four. (We know from *Dr. Bob and the Good Oldtimers* that this member later had several slips.)

AA today is more receptive than ever to young people, and the young people who went before us lovingly paved the way to make it a smoother journey. I am one of the many who joined AA in the late 1960s and early 1970s. We were in our late teens and early twenties then, and most of us have been continuously clean, sober, and active since. But old stereotypes and attitudes die hard. Many AA members (including some young newcomers themselves) mistakenly believe that young AAs automatically have high bottoms or aren't "real" alcoholics to begin with. One man told me his reaction to this stereotype when he joined AA thirteen years ago as a young, angry, broke, divorced, sick, unemployed, homeless, ex-convict alcoholic: "You mean I have to be old, too?"

Even the Big Book states, "We, who are familiar with the symptoms, see large numbers of potential alcoholics among young people everywhere. But try to get them to see it!" The idea that young people were not real alcoholics or had not suffered enough yet was continued in *Twelve Steps and Twelve Traditions*, as it describes the emergence into AA of "young people who were scarcely more than potential alcoholics. They were spared that last ten or fifteen years of literal hell the rest of us had gone through."

We always had a good laugh at that passage in the Step study group I belonged to. An old-timer gave one of our members a suspicious glance and said, "I probably spilled more than you ever drank." Our friend's response: "Maybe that's why I got here so young. I rarely spilled any, and if I did, I licked it up."

Of course, the vast majority of older members were delighted with our entrance into AA and enthusiastically supported our efforts at recovery. Actually, the point of that *Twelve Steps and Twelve Traditions* passage was to let high-bottom types of all ages know they are welcome in AA, and the Big Book statement has been footnoted: "True when this book was published. But a 1983 U.S./Canada membership survey showed about one-fifth of AAs were 30 and under."*

Many of these newcomers are half the age of those who have traditionally been considered AA's "young people." Teen and preteen drinking is a growing problem, and some of these young drinkers are appearing at meetings. It is too easy for such young members to be patronized, ignored, or not taken seriously. Even in young people's groups, the fourteen-year-old newcomers may, other than alcoholism, have less in common with the twenty-eight-year-olds there than the twenty-eight-year-olds have with the forty-five-year-old members at other AA meetings.

So there are now teen AA groups (not Alateen groups) being formed separately from young people's groups. Some young people's round-ups offer "under twenty-one" meetings to help the teenage newcomer identify. More and more young people's committees are springing up to throw dances and to show teenagers that recovery can be fun. The third edition of the Big Book includes "A Teen-Ager's Decision," a story about a girl who joined AA when she was eighteen. Pamphlets aimed at teenage alcoholics are appearing at more and more meetings. Ironically, young people's groups need to face up to the fact that the true young people in AA today are probably ten- to twenty-year-old children and adolescents, not twenty-five- to forty-year-old adults.

In any event, there is an increasing pool of young people in AA who, by demographic fact alone, will eventually become the old-timers and elder statesmen and women of the Fellowship. Some of these young newcomers will remain sober but inactive in AA, and others will drop out, relapse, and die. But many will stay to share their recovery with others and will go on to become the backbone of our service efforts down through the years.

How can we help today's young people prepare for this responsibility? Perhaps we can begin by setting the same example of service for these teenage newcomers that the older members set for me when I first joined AA. From coffeemaker to delegate, there is something for everyone in AA service. And service work is as essential to recovery as it is to AA's longevity.

Most of the AAs who introduced me and my contemporaries to service work were older, experienced members who took quiet delight in tending to AA's future. They were much more interested in our commitment to AA than in our age, hairstyle, clothes, language, or other problems and addictions. Our sobriety and willingness to serve was all it took for them to entrust us with increasing service responsibilities when we proved capable and ready. They taught us, when we found it difficult to let go of positions because "no one else would do it," that we should create vacuums so they could be filled. They showed us that we don't have to be in a hurry to hold every service office, because there will always be something for us to rotate into. These old-timers also taught us that practicing these principles in all our affairs meant that overcommitment to service work could indicate a shirking of family and other responsibilities; but no involvement in service work meant that our sobriety could be shaky and that we weren't doing our part to make sure AA is around to carry the message to future generations of alcoholics.

When we sobered up, the older people in AA sponsored us into service in young people's groups. Many of us started as tagalongs, observers, and alternates for the intergroup and general service offices we would eventually hold. Under the direction of more experienced members, we learned those traits of responsibility, punctuality, follow-through, and compromise that now serve us so well in our business and home lives.

With the maturity and experience gained from the older members, we then rotated into "mainstream" AA service responsibilities. In our experience, young people who restrict their Twelfth Step and service work to other young people and young people's groups alone do not experience the full healing power of Alcoholics Anonymous and deny themselves and others the opportunity to work with AAs of all ages.

So more and more people with experience in young people's groups are becoming general service representatives, district committee members, and even delegates. As that great friend of AA, Bernard B. Smith, so eloquently described it on page 281 of *Alcoholics Anonymous Comes of Age*: "We may not need a General Service Conference to insure our own recovery. But we do need it to insure the recovery of the alcoholic who still stumbles in the darkness, seeking the light. We need it to insure the recovery of some newborn child, inexplicably destined to alcoholism. We need it to provide, in keeping with the Twelfth Step, a permanent haven for all alcoholics who in the ages ahead can find in AA that rebirth which brought its first members back to life."

Many of us "young people" in AA today were the newborn children Bernard Smith spoke of. We smile as our wrinkles, gray hairs, and AA birthdays multiply. (One young man has a receding hairline, but prefers to think that God likes his face so much he's making it bigger.) We owe eternal gratitude to those AA members whose efforts were responsible for keeping AA alive for us when we needed it. We can do no less for the legions of young people now joining AA.

P. C.
Del Mar, California
May 1986

* *The General Service Conference is the method by which AA's collective group conscience can speak forcefully and put its desires for services such as the publication of AA literature into effect in North America. This structure ensures that the full voice of AA can be heard.*

ICYPAA Bounces Back

In the Big Book, AAs are compared to "passengers of a great liner the moment after rescue from shipwreck when camaraderie, joyousness and democracy pervade the vessel from steerage to Captain's table." From June 30 to July 2, 2006, the Sheraton Hotel in New Orleans was such a vessel.

Only here, the great majority of passengers were in their teens, twenties, and thirties.

Each year, the International Conference of Young People in Alcoholics Anonymous, or ICYPAA (pronounced "ick-ee-pa"), holds a conference that feels like a party – a good party – without the hangover, blackout, or shame. Since 1958, ICYPAA has met on an annual basis and in a different city each year. And everyone, everyone, is welcome.

The purpose of ICYPAA, as its statement of purpose says, is to "carry AA's message of recovery and to provide a setting for an annual celebration of sobriety among young people in AA."

Why is it so important to celebrate in sobriety? As one young woman from Louisiana said, "You're kidding, right?" With a delighted laugh, she quoted from the text of *Alcoholics Anonymous*: "If newcomers could see no joy or fun in our existence, they wouldn't want it." At ICYPAA, there was lots of joy and lots of fun. She grasped my hand, flashed me a smile, and pulled me across the room to meet some of her friends.

The ICYPAA schedule of events spanned Thursday to Sunday with late-night meetings, an old-timers' ice-cream social, panel discussions (on such topics as getting sober at eighteen and under), bidding information, a Q&A with GSO, and dancing and live music until early morning hours.

On Thursday, the Pre-Conference Event kicked off at the recently reopened Aquarium of the Americas. AAs wound through the aquarium for exotic views of maritime flora and fauna. Penguins played in a simulation of their natural habitat and charmed their audience. Over plates of jambalaya, AAs hailed old friends, met new ones, and brought them along to the 10:30 P.M. speaker meeting in the Napoleon Ballroom to finish off the evening.

By Friday, most ICYPAA attendees had arrived from all over the United States and Canada – others traveled from as far as Ireland and New Zealand. Participants had their pick of an emotional sobriety workshop, panel discussions, and various information seminars. That evening, Holly H., from Lake Charles, Louisiana, shared about being young in AA. "If you're new to AA and you're looking for a relationship or a better job, you'll probably find it," she said. The crowd tittered, and seemed to recall some of their early desires when first walking through AA's doors. Holly continued, "But if you're looking for sobriety, you're going to find that, too." At this, the young assembled AAs cheered heartily and loud. That, they seemed to say, was what we were looking for all along.

On Saturday evening, young AAs, suited up and slicked-down, entered the Armstrong Ballroom to share a banquet dinner. Later, conference attendees were surprised with a Mardi Gras parade – a brightly painted float circled the Napoleon Ballroom while masked AAs threw beaded necklaces and doubloons. The Cajun beat rocked the crowd and bounced off the rafters, as ICYPAAs jumped and stretched to catch the beads rocketing colorfully through the air. When all the beads had been caught and most of the jumping had died down, the sobriety countdown began. By the time AAs began to stand and claim their thirty days, twenty days, ten days, ICYPAA attendees were cheering with a fevered pitch of love and excitement. It was easy to get the message – there is joy, fun, and life in sobriety.

Carlston, from Shreveport, Louisiana, got sober at seventeen. Not long after, he was taken to an ICYPAA and returned home better prepared to carry the message of recovery to others. How did an ICYPAA help? "There was something there that I wanted," he said. "People my age were having a ball. I thought I'd have to give up fun when I got sober." Now in his twentieth year of sobriety, Carlston serves as the chair of the ICYPAA48 Louisiana host committee. "This has been a powerful experience for me," he said. "The guys on the Louisiana host committee thought they were bringing a conference for young people to New Orleans – they thought they'd be doing service for a year. Then, Katrina blew through. Many of our guys didn't have homes to go to. They lost their jobs and everything they had. But they showed up to do another year of conference planning and work, all over again. And do you know what they said? They said: 'This is my service commitment to AA.'"

"You know," Carlston continued, "they didn't even know they were doing anything special."

Mike, from Connecticut, has been coming to ICYPAA for over twenty years to reconnect with old AA friends. He was surrounded by sober drunks whose happy looks and demeanor were no different from the teens' and twenty-somethings' milling about. Except, perhaps, that salt and pepper spiced their hair and most sported laugh lines. When asked why they kept coming back, many answered, "Haven't missed one since 1993," or 1987, or even 1972. This is, of course, a testament to the enjoyment of ICYPAA, but what is it about ICYPAA that keeps AAs coming back once they are no longer considered "young people"?

"This is AA!" claimed Reed from North Carolina. At my quizzical look, he continued, "I didn't even know it, but I was dying. I held off from doing service work for young people's AA for the longest time – I figured, it's not for me. I attended a service meeting just to get someone off my back and I walked out with a service position for young people's AA in my area. And wouldn't you know it? The quality of my sobriety went straight up. I knew happiness." He paused a moment and looked out across the hotel lobby. In view were quiet greetings, hearty handshakes, shrieks of laughter, and a long line for iced coffee. "There is passion here, and friendliness, and a desire for the message of recovery. I am looking forward to meeting friends, old and new. For me, this is AA."

Marathon Meetings, a staple at ICYPAA, are a good way to meet friends. Meetings ran from 12:00 A.M. on Friday, to 10:00 A.M. Sunday. Each meeting had a quote or topic, pre-selected from AA literature, to use as a springboard. One meeting discussed what AAs can expect as a result of completing the Fifth Step. "We can look the world in the eye. We can be alone at perfect peace and ease. Our fears fall from us. We begin to feel the nearness of our Creator."

Sharing, at first slow and faltering, picked up speed as young AAs shared their experience with the Fifth Step. One young man shared that being at ICYPAA was great – amazing, he said. "But I don't have the problems in 'older people' AA that I do in young people's AA." He explained, "I am not self-conscious around the older folks; I can go for coffee, chat after a meeting, and feel perfectly relaxed and unself-conscious. But, when I walk into a group of people my own age, I start thinking, Oh, man, they've got more than me — they're better-looking, they have more money, they are more confident — I'm afraid they won't accept me. It feels like walking into the high school cafeteria, and it brings my fears front and center. I'm here working through it — what I get is more than fun, it's hope and knowledge about myself."

Service opportunities are plentiful at a conference or convention, and ICYPAA48 was no exception. Louisiana host committee volunteers greeted cheerfully, while directions, safety, security, and a host of other unseen needs were taken care of by other committee members.

Each year, in a different city, local young AAs are provided with a great opportunity to carry the message to "new friends in your own community. . . . If you live in a large place, there are hundreds. High and low, rich and poor, these are future fellows of Alcoholics Anonymous. Among them you will make lifelong friends." To the AAs involved, the joy, fellowship, and opportunities involved in hosting an ICYPAA may bring the message of recovery to someone who, like themselves, thought that sobriety would be a glum and miserable existence.

According to the long-time AAs living it up, ICYPAA is not only for teenagers and twenty-somethings. "Hey, we used to say it is for the young. Now, we like to say it is for the young-at-heart. Actually, though, it is for anyone who is still open and willing."

October 2006

The Opportunity to Change

I walked through the doors of Alcoholics Anonymous when I was fifteen. When I first started drinking, it was fun. Then it was fun and problems. Then it turned out to be just problems. The first time I got drunk, I was thirteen years old. I blacked out and don't remember much. But what I do remember is that I felt like King Kong, bigger and badder than everyone else. I became the center of attention.

I continued to drink and get in trouble. I drank mostly on weekends. I was known to kids I drank with as "the alcoholic." For some reason I just couldn't have a few beers like everyone else did. I had to have twelve, fifteen, or sometimes twenty-four.

My drinking got really bad toward the end, and I admitted myself to a ten-day inpatient treatment center. Unfortunately, I didn't leave there with hope, and I stayed dry for only five weeks. I hit my bottom on March 28, 1996. The next day, I made my first Alcoholics Anonymous meeting. I don't remember much from that meeting, but I do remember leaving that meeting with a lot of hope. I also remember how the people around the tables said to keep coming back.

I've been coming back for the year and a half that I've been a member of AA. I've seen a lot of changes in my life. I do a lot of Twelfth Step work and encourage younger kids to become involved with AA. Today, my primary purpose is to stay sober and help another alcoholic to achieve sobriety. I am so grateful to my Higher Power and the Fellowship of Alcoholics Anonymous that I've been blessed with the opportunity to change my life.

Dean P.
Highland, Indiana
February 1998

Miles of Smiles

When I first came to the program, I was scared and ashamed and alone. At my first meeting, there were only a couple of women and no young people. Being a young college student who had not lost anything substantial (I had nothing to lose at that point in my life), I felt as though I did not meet the requirements for being an alcoholic.

After going home that morning and drinking, I felt guilty. So the next day, I went to another meeting with the hope of finding people who would tell me that I was not an alcoholic.

There were ten or fifteen people close to my age at the meeting. In my mind I was like, "Oh-oh. Young people can be alcoholics, too." That is when my denial started to show up: I did not have time for ninety meetings in ninety days. I was not going to read any Big Book written in my grandfather's time. I was not going to talk to women because they were all mean. And I had already done these Steps in another program.

I talked the talk, but I did not walk the walk, and sure enough I ended up drinking once again. I remember that night as if it were yesterday. I remember lying on my bed, unable to move, wishing that I would die. I was worthless. There was no hope for me in this world. Then, I prayed to this God I knew, and I asked him to kill me unless he could show me a better way of life.

The next day I woke up to the phone ringing. It was my aunt from New York calling to let me know that my uncle had died the night before. I went to the house of a person in AA who suggested that I go to a meeting. I was scared. Who would want a drunk like me at an AA meeting? But I went back to that meeting and another one later that night. The next day, I went to a Big Book study, asked this woman to be my sponsor, and began to work the program of Alcoholics Anonymous. Just about a month into my sobriety, my sponsor told me that I needed to get into service work. (I should let you know that I call my sponsor a service freak because she does it all the time.) I gave her a reason why I could not do anything, and she gave me a better reason why I should: You have to give it away to keep it.

I went to a young people's camp-out that weekend and learned that on Sunday they were having an ICYPAA bid committee meeting. I planned to go just to tell my sponsor that I went, so she'd be happy. I walked out of there as the co-secretary. I was stunned. I went home, called my sponsor right away, and told her what had happened. Then I went out and mailed postcards to everyone on the committee reminding them of our next meeting.

Every time I went to a committee meeting, people met me with smiles on their faces, said hello to me as I came in, and made me feel welcome. As time wore on, I looked forward to seeing their smiles and enjoying the friendships I was building with them.

Later in my sobriety, my sponsor strongly suggested that I attend one of our area meetings, since it was in my hometown that month. Grudgingly, I went. I was sitting there listening to people having heated debates over things like smoking and food. I looked at my sponsor and vowed that I was never going to come back to one of these meetings. As I was getting ready to walk out, an area officer stopped me and said, "Hi." Before I knew it, we were having a conversation over lunch. When the meeting was over and I was leaving, a few of the area officers asked if I was going to be there next month. Before I knew it, the word "yes" slipped out of my mouth, and there I was the next month.

No, I really did not want to go. So what made me return? The smiles. After that first day, people made me feel a part of and not apart from everyone else, despite the fact that most of them were old enough to be my parents or older. And it was all because of one little smile and the famous words, "Keep coming back."

Today I keep going back, and I actually look forward to seeing their smiling faces each month. I have met people in service work all across the States, and I think that it is awesome. I only hope that the next person who walks through the doors will be able to see the smiles on our faces and want to keep coming back, too.

Emily B.
Grand Rapids, Michigan
January 2001

From *Sobriety Rocks!*, *March 1998*

A A co-founder Bill W. was convinced of the power of young people to carry the message when he met some young people in New York. Here is part of a 1968 letter he wrote (quoted in the March 1971 memorial issue of the Grapevine): "Some weeks ago, there was a young people's convention of AAs. Shortly thereafter, four of these kids visited the office. I saw one young gal prancing down the hall, hair flying, in a mini-skirt, wearing love beads, and the works. I thought, 'Holy smoke, what now?' She told me she was the oldest member of the young people's group in her area — age twenty-two! They had kids as young as sixteen. I was curious and took the whole party out to lunch.

"Well, they were absolutely wonderful. They talked (and acted) just about as good a kind of AA as I've seen anywhere. I think all of them said they had had some kind of drug problem, but had kicked that, too. When they first came around, they had insisted on their own ideas of AA, but in the end they found AA plenty good enough as it was. Though they needed their own meetings, they found interest and inspiration in the meetings of much older folks as well."

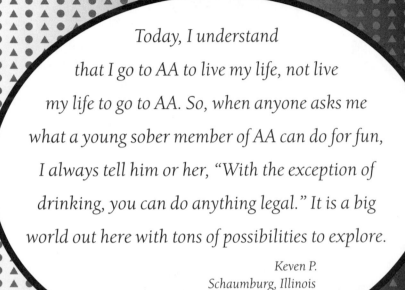

Today, I understand that I go to AA to live my life, not live my life to go to AA. So, when anyone asks me what a young sober member of AA can do for fun, I always tell him or her, "With the exception of drinking, you can do anything legal." It is a big world out here with tons of possibilities to explore.

Keven P.
Schaumburg, Illinois

Section Seven: **HAPPY, JOYOUS, AND REAL**

Rock 'n' Roll Sobriety

I was very apprehensive but decided to loosen up a bit and go to the rock concert anyway. I felt I had grown out of a lot of that loud, deafening music, but since my sister really wanted me to go I agreed. What the hell, I was still young — twenty-three years old that is, and flexible enough to fit in with just about any group of people. I decided to make it a good time so I threw out my negative feelings and geared myself with a positive attitude. Thus was my mental state when I headed for the Riverfest on Harriet Island to rock with REO Speedwagon.

We got there early enough to get good seats, and I sat back to observe the throngs of people who filed past. Their eyes sparkled with anticipation and their faces gave evidence of the excitement they felt. Raw energy hung low like a heavy fog and mixed with the warm, damp air left over from the muggy day. Multicolored, greased-up hair, six-inch chain earrings, black leather studded outfits, and bright, bold, colorful sunglasses caught my eye. Nothing was unexpected, however. I was merely a spectator enjoying the show as my continuous grin would suggest to those passing by.

The concert was finally getting under way and my friends needed more beer, so off they trotted to battle the crowds and long lines while I attempted to save their seats. Of course they missed the first song and almost lost their seats. While I was dancing and clapping to the music, I could see them off in the distance as they jostled their way through the crowd, trying to save their sacred beer from spillage. It seemed an eternity, but everyone finally settled in.

By this time, the band was working up a sweat and the crowd's intense energy was growing. It didn't take long before the familiar smell of marijuana played on my senses. Oh, God! I decided right then and there to thank God for my sobriety. It seemed only yesterday when at this same concert I was too stoned to even realize what songs were played. Hard rock is tough to figure out anyway, yet at least tonight my mind was intact and

142

I could actually distinguish one instrument from the next and figure out the rhythm.

Unfortunately my enthusiastic, absorbed state was interrupted. "What d'ya want?" I screamed at my sister over the grating sound of heavy metal.

"We have to go to the bathroom," she yelled. I had forgotten that wretched curse of beer drinking.

"Okay," I shouted, "but hurry back. I can't be saving seats all night." Off they went again while I continued to enjoy the show. Yes, by God, I was enjoying this concert.

All around me people were losing their balance and falling off benches because of the effects of alcohol and drugs. Yet I firmly held my ground and confidently stepped up my movements in the tiny spot I inhabited. I was amazed at the amount of control I felt amid all this unleashed energy. Sweating bodies were pushed and shoved in the whirlwind of mass chaos, while endless screaming mingled in the air with pounding drums and electrifying acoustics – still, I was in control! My thoughts were soon disturbed by the scrawny kid next to me.

"Do you have an extra joint?"

"What?" I exclaimed, clearly flabbergasted. He was maybe fifteen or sixteen.

"Do you have any extra weed, man?" he repeated, somewhat hesitant this time.

"I wouldn't even have a match to light one for you," I answered. He didn't seem to believe me, but I really couldn't help him. I looked at him again and smiled.

Half an hour passed before I saw the familiar faces of my sister and her friends. They were having trouble getting through the wild crowd. Too bad they were missing the whole show. When they finally made it, I informed her that they had played her favorite song. "Don't go to the bathroom," she shouted in my ear, uninterested in my comment. "You wouldn't believe how long the lines are."

As she continued to be preoccupied with lighting her cigarette and carefully guarding what beer she had salvaged, I absorbed myself in the excitement of the live music and the fact that I was seeing — really seeing — REO Speedwagon for the first time.

The thoughts and emotions that coursed through me that night are almost inexpressible. I recognized a year and a half of growth amid the blaring, screeching, deafening sounds of electric guitars and synthesizers, and saw for the first time that this was what self-esteem was all about. I was not afraid to do my own thing in this crowd. I was not worried about how I looked, nor intimidated by how others looked. I was not comparing myself to others; I was not crazy and felt no need to act crazy; I was definitely not unhappy; and I was not thirsting for attention and acceptance or trying so hard to feel that I belonged. I was not inside looking out, rather I was outside looking in.

I stood in the middle of 35,000 people and felt free to be a different, unique individual. The most important part of it all is that my Higher Power was with me and I was conscious of him. How many other people in this rowdy, rambunctious crowd were thinking of a God and feeling the greater effects of his energy and power? How many times while I was drinking did I become conscious of my Higher Power and my inner feelings? I can't think of one. The only times I remember being aware of that is when I cried out in pain and desperation. He was there then, but I couldn't see him through my tears, my darkness, my raw pain.

"Did you have a good time?" I asked my sister when it was all over.

"Yeah, it was great," she answered but quickly changed the subject to the amount of beer that was spilled on her. I could plainly see the effects of the concert were short-lived. Tomorrow she would not remember the real music, only a loud, indistinguishable sound and a lot of people. I, however, had discovered a new dimension to my sobriety, and it was well worth a hard-earned six bucks!

B. Z.
St. Paul, Minnesota
May 1986

The Cup of Life

We have a saying in AA where I live: "Looking for a relationship in AA is like shopping for a new car in a wrecker's yard!" Not only recovering alcoholics but all sorts of emotionally immature people can make impulsive blunders in the relationship area. But the price they pay for relationship folly usually does not include insanity and death! Hence AA's caution not to start relationships in the first year of recovery that is urged upon newcomers.

Sure it's hard having to "do life" guided by a higher set of principles than nonrecovering folk can get by on, damn hard! But the Big Book says, "Yes, there is a long period of reconstruction ahead" and that must be our primary purpose in AA — not bedding that luscious newcomer! The wonderful thing about AA is that with so many warm friendships of both genders available, the pressure I felt while drinking to find someone, anyone, to go to bed with became much less intense. My sex life finally became manageable! But in early sobriety, I remember moaning to another member about how I didn't have a relationship, I didn't have a new car, and I didn't have a flashy job. He replied: "It takes a steady hand to hold a full cup!" Instantly, I knew where my priorities lay. I would be best served by focusing not on what God had put (or had not) in my cup of life, but on the need to steady my juvenile demands for instant and full gratification.

Older AA members never fill the nervous newcomers' cups of coffee to the brim for much the same reason: They could spill it, make a big fool of themselves, and never come back!

Graham M.
Canberra, Australia
February 2003

The Most Beautiful Word in the English Language

There is a line on page 133 in the Big Book that states: "We are sure that God wants us to be happy, joyous and free." I'd like to tell you about the happiness, the joy, and the freedom I've been granted since I was released from the compulsion to drink.

I came into Alcoholics Anonymous on Valentine's Day 1988 and I wanted what you all had, but I judged myself unworthy of the kindness and love shown to me. I knew I was sick and that I hurt; but I had lost all hope of ever getting better. Hope is something that comes to us all at different times during our journey on the AA path. Some find it instantly while others find it along the way.

I found hope after almost a month of wandering in and out of meetings in a zombie-like state. For weeks I had heard announcements of some upcoming event called "ISCYPAA," but I had no idea what "ISCYPAA" was and was afraid to ask. Besides, I couldn't even pronounce it! Lucky for me someone asked me if I was going. I swallowed my pride and asked what it was. The Illinois State Conference of Young People in AA was the answer I got.

Well, that sounded good (I was eighteen years old at the time), so I decided to go for the day and see what it was all about.

A week later I went alone to this hotel a few miles from my home. But I wasn't alone: there were 1,500 young alcoholics running around this balloon-filled hotel! I was terrified! Everyone seemed to know everyone else and I felt kind of silly and left out. To make matters worse, I still didn't know how to pronounce all those letters.

But, my Higher Power, whom I choose to call God, was looking out for me. I met some incredibly friendly people who took me to meetings and showed me around for the first few hours.

I didn't have a room, but I didn't care. For the first time in my life I was starting to relax without having to drink. Everyone I met gave me hugs, smiles, and made me laugh. I called my mother and told her I was going to stay the night, because I didn't want to leave all the nice people at the conference. I was starting to blend in with the rest of the people, going to meetings and drinking coffee. I was feeling very good.

Sometime around two o'clock in the morning I found myself standing by a coffee urn getting my umpteenth cup of coffee, when I saw a man standing beside me. He was blocking the cream containers, so I asked him to pass me one. He passed me the cream and told me his name was Steve S.

We got into a discussion about AA and sobriety. It was Steve who, by his joy, showed me that the most beautiful word in the English language is "sober." On the stairs leading to the roof of this hotel in Napierville, Illinois, I was granted the hope promised to me by all the members I'd spoken to. It was Steve's simple love and respect for the AA way of life that showed me living sober was a glorious way to live. I wanted what he had. I wanted the joy, the freedom, and the happiness he was showing me by how he lived. That night I took the First, Second and Third Steps in my heart.

All that night and into the next day we shared and listened to each other. The conference was only for a weekend; it couldn't last forever. I was sad when it ended, but happy to discover Steve lived only half an hour from my home! We exchanged phone numbers.

Through the meetings and my sponsors I have found the joy that Steve had shown me the night we met. I understand that joy comes from living the way my conscience tells me to live. Joy comes from celebrating being sober this twenty-four hours and humbly realizing my sobriety is a gift from God to me. Freedom is being liberated from the desire to drink and being given a new life through the Steps. Freedom is being able to choose not to drink today and knowing that I have that choice. Happiness is sudden laughter bubbling from my heart to my mouth because I know that I've been given a present so wonderful that there are no words to describe it.

Yes, I can be happy, joyous, and free today – right now! And it isn't the kind of happiness that leaves me sick the next morning. It isn't the kind of joy that makes me wonder what I did the night before. And it isn't the kind of freedom that can be bought or sold. It is simply a gift. No matter what happens, this serenity, this inner joy remains.

But I don't mean I'm living on a cloud somewhere, because I'm not! Pain is part of being alive; it's how well I accept and cope that determines the level of joy in my life. Friends die unexpectedly, but I don't drink. Plans have a tendency to fall through, but I don't drink.

Not drinking is the first requirement for joy; the second requirement is gratitude. Steve taught me that – through his actions, not his words. He attracted me to Alcoholics Anonymous at that conference because of how he lived. Steve was a picture from the Big Book, walking proof that the Steps work.

So here it is, sixteen months since we met in front of a coffeepot and in eighty days, Steve and I are getting married! We are living and loving each other because of the gift of sobriety.

Marie C.
Lombard, Illinois
February 1995

Firm Bedrock

In the Big Book, the section on sex comes right after the section on fear. It took me a long time to see how fear and sex were woven together in my life.

When I first got sober, the Big Book's idea about taking inventory about sex seemed simple enough. You put each relationship to the test: was it selfish or not? Gradually, that question became more difficult to answer, as my life got further away from drinking and more information came into my awareness.

I began to realize that perhaps I had some grave emotional and mental disorders. This sex business was much more complicated than it seemed at first. I had been sexually abused by my father and others. I am a lesbian. Drinking and sex were connected from the beginning, and once I started my own drinking, I left a huge trail of sexual wreckage. I did tremendous harm to myself and others.

There came a point in my sobriety when all I could figure out about sex was to stop doing it completely. The only thing that I knew for sure about God's will for me was that God wanted me to stay sober. My sponsor set an example for me by making it very clear that our relationship was to be absolutely nonsexual. I imitated her when I became a sponsor, and those relationships taught me a tremendous amount about love without sex.

At four and a half years sober, I was diagnosed with multiple personality disorder. I began to learn about taking responsibility for my behavior in a much more complete way. I put Alcoholics Anonymous firmly at the base of my recovery, and it was the one thing that I could always fall back on. I prayed a lot. I had a lot of therapy. I felt consumed by the enormity of dealing with my past, my childhood, my feelings and imaginings, my bitterness and resentment. I felt sure that I could never have a normal intimate relationship, and I was filled with despair and anger.

AA was my bedrock. It was the only thing that I was sure of, the only thing that I knew was good for me. Members of my home group heard me talk week after week from the depths of despair. I showed up at meetings no matter what, and held onto them for my life and my sanity. I kept it as simple as I could. The only value I could see in what I was going through was that I was truly able to be understanding and compassionate to others with similar backgrounds. I could empathize with their experience, and demonstrate that it was possible to stay sober. I didn't drink, and an amazing thing happened. It all began to pass. The clouds lifted. Things cleared. I began sleeping through the night. I began to feel that I was healing. I had good days. I became interested in life again.

At nine years sober, I fell in love. I found myself in a relationship that meant the world to me. It was time to take a good look at sex and sobriety. The line in the Big Book which has helped me the most is in the chapter "How It Works": "Whatever our ideal turns out to be, we must be willing to grow toward it." It took me a long time to begin to see what my ideal might turn out to be. Now that I have a pretty good idea of that, I work hard on my willingness to grow toward it.

I am blessed with a partner who loves me deeply. Although she cannot understand or relate to the terrors that I sometimes have around sex and intimacy, she is patient and loving and gives me the room to find myself, step by step.

I no longer pray to have my fear removed. Today, I pray that my love grows bigger than my fear and that my humility becomes greater than my shame. On the days when I can say these prayers honestly, along with my daily prayer to do no harm, my sexual life is beyond my wildest dreams.

Recovery is possible, life is sweet, and drinking is the farthest thing from my mind.

Anonymous
May 1999

The Bright Spot

I went to my first AA meeting at the age of sixteen. On the outside, I tried to project the image of confidence. On the inside, I was dying. I put on a tough attitude to keep people away. I was afraid if they really could see through me that they would just confirm what I already thought. I hated who I was and what I had become and I just wanted it to be over. I prayed many nights to God, asking him to kill me in my sleep, always saying that I would do it myself in the morning if he didn't. The next day I'd get up and just start drinking.

When I walked into my first meeting, I didn't know what to expect. Maybe they would teach me how to control my drinking. I had no idea that they would tell me complete abstinence. I heard one thing at my first meeting: "One was too many and a thousand were never enough." I instantly related. That was true for me.

I looked around the rooms and saw a lot of "old" people. There was one other teenager besides myself at the meetings and I knew that he wasn't completely abstinent. I listened to the stories and I saw all the differences. I didn't lose a house, job, or husband. A woman told me not to look for the differences but for the similarities. I may not have been old enough to have lost a house or job or husband, but when I got honest with myself I had lost the trust of my parents, been suspended from school, kicked out of band, and been picked up for being a runaway. I did feel empty, suicidal, and full of fear. I focused a lot on my age since I was only a teenager. How was I going to stay sober the rest of my life? I had no idea how to live without alcohol or drugs. I'd forgotten what life was like before I picked up. I couldn't remember what I was supposed to go back to or how I should spend my time. Drinking and drugging had become my life and now that I was sober, I had no idea what to do. I was on a rollercoaster of emotions. I reacted to everything and nothing. I showed up for a meeting at the last minute and left right way when it was over. I didn't talk to people, I didn't share in meetings, and I was miserable.

I started dating an old drinking buddy. He was still active and I was tempted. He didn't like the fact that I went to meetings. He kept saying I was meeting other guys there.

A couple of months later, I was faced with a dilemma – I knew that either I get rid of the boyfriend or I would drink. I gave up the boyfriend and found myself sitting in a meeting with my hand raised to share. That, for me, was my First Step. I was finally reaching out for help and being willing to go to any length to get it. For the first time, I knew I didn't want to drink and I couldn't do it by myself, I needed the people in these rooms. I showed up early to set up for meetings. I stayed after and put chairs and ashtrays away. I went out for coffee after the meetings and listened and watched how sober people acted. I became a coffee drinker.

I was still attending high school and felt very alone there. Occasionally, a classmate would join the Fellowship for a while, but it didn't last long.

The love of the Fellowship got me through those lonely times at school. On graduation night my home group threw me a party and it was awesome. I didn't know how I was going to do that sober and they showed me. I got involved in service work and that introduced me to a lot more people and sober events. The Fellowship became the bright spot of my life. This was my beginning.

I have learned so many things in recovery. I think the most important thing was I learned how to love myself and trust in God. I didn't have to have the bottle or the drugs to feel pretty and good. I don't feel like I want to die today and I definitely don't hate who I am anymore. It is because of the Fellowship and God and the Steps. The Fellowship loved me until I could learn to use God and the Steps to love myself, and for that I will be eternally grateful.

Young people do recover and it is always a joy to see teenagers come to meetings. It reminds me of me. When I got sober, I was told that the recovery rate for teenagers was zero. That wasn't very encouraging. I just kept coming back and coming back and coming back. No matter what, I didn't drink or drug. They told me not to drink even if my behind fell off. They said to bring it to a meeting and they would sew it back on. That is true, and they did. I was sober on my twenty-first birthday. What a miracle that was. I remember being so afraid because now I was really legal drinking age. I went to a meeting and shared. I was complicating the whole thing. Someone asked, "Do you want to drink?" and I said, "No." It was just that simple.

I just celebrated eighteen years without a drink or drug and I'm so grateful. On page 164, the Big Book says, "See to it that your relationship with Him is right, and great events will come to pass for you and countless others. This is the Great Fact for us." Great events have happened for me in sobriety and I have also witnessed great events come to pass for others. I have a wonderful marriage, a wonderful daughter, and I'm glad to be alive and sober. Without God, AA, and especially the Steps, I wouldn't have any of it. A sponsor once told me, "Place credit where credit is due, and it's not with you." That is keeping it simple for me.

Cheryl O.
Niceville, Florida
October 2004

The Band Played On

During my childhood, I struggled with alcoholism's symptoms of isolation, loneliness, feeling different, and having a fantasy world to escape to when real life got too tough. During my teens, I struggled with the progressive symptoms of drinking to excess, blackouts, and drug abuse, along with the childhood symptoms that were still there. I also developed anorexia and bulimia.

During my twenties, I struggled with all of the above symptoms, and most of the symptoms got worse. By age twenty-seven, I had been through psychotherapy, psychiatric hospitalization, a three-day stay at Beatrice House in Los Angeles, and, finally, my first alcoholism treatment center in San Diego. At last, I had found Alcoholics Anonymous.

Ironically, during my twenties, I also managed to graduate from college in Boston with a degree in public communications and some high ambitions. It seems that all through my life, I was living on two parallel tracks: on one track I was headed for an illustrious recording career, and on the other track I was headed for a wall. I started a rock band with a close friend from college, and we recruited band members who believed in our music and our ideals. Soon after we graduated, we had a band that in our innocence we had great hopes for. Little did we realize that alcohol and drugs would destroy our band, our friendships, and even one of our lives.

After a brief stint as a radio announcer (where I trashed yet another promising career because of my arrogance), I moved back to my home town of Los Angeles to join my friends who had migrated out there. We reformed our band with two new members, and started gigging. Incredibly, we landed a record deal with a record label that wanted to take a chance on us and our music. These were heady times. I remember thinking, as I set up my synthesizer in the dark womb of the recording studio, that I finally felt "safe," as if nothing could touch me in the studio and all that mattered was the music. But there I was, racing along, side by side with myself on those parallel tracks, one headed for glory and the other headed for the wall. Our guitar player, who was also my boyfriend, was with me on the track headed straight for the wall.

As we recorded the album, the booze and the drugs flowed, and we felt invincible. Parts of the album were even pretty good, and I'm still proud of my work. Yet all the while, something insidious was happening. The close group of friends from college had lost its innocence and was turning on itself. The friendships were becoming fragmented by the insanity of the booze and drugs, only we were blaming the discord on "artistic differences." My guitar player and I had descended into the hell of heroin addiction, and the rest of the band chastised us for being "junkies," while they righteously snorted their cocaine. When the album was finally released, we had one hit single from it, but the album never really took off. The record company finally dropped our contract, and we were left with nothing. Soon afterward, our drummer was in a motorcycle accident and suffered head injuries that severely altered his life. And the band gradually fell apart.

My guitar player and I struggled with our habits for the next couple of years. When I was introduced to AA, I knew right away that I belonged, but I couldn't leave my guitar player to get sober. So I remained in my own personal hell. It wasn't until we lost or sold everything we had, went on methadone for the umpteenth time, and came back to Boston on a Greyhound bus, that we finally escaped the drugs. It was a geographical cure that worked on one level, but I continued to drink around the clock.

Finally, my guitar player left me. He knew that if I didn't get sober I would die, and he wasn't ready to get sober. When he left me, I finally lost my last excuse. I was twenty-nine years old, and my life was in ruins. I returned to Alcoholics Anonymous, and this time (as it says in Step One of the "Twelve and Twelve"), I was "as open-minded to conviction and as willing to listen as the dying can be." I haven't found it necessary to pick up a drink for over five years now.

My first year of sobriety was spent clearing up and cleaning up the mess. I had no solid place to live, I was heavily in debt, and my family had effectively detached from me. I got myself a sponsor (actually two sponsors because they were a couple, so I had every base covered!). They told me to get into the Twelve Steps, which I did, in my first month of sobriety. If it wasn't for the Steps, I would not have been able to deal with the massive amounts of damage left by my alcoholism. I believe that it's never too early for the Steps, because the point is to try and practice them to the best of our ability, not to master them when we think we are "well enough" to truly understand them all! During my first Eighth and Ninth Steps, I was able to make arrangements to pay back the money I owed on a payment schedule, and by eighteen months sober, I had paid back all my debts. I started temping as a secretary at one month sober; by six months sober my Higher Power (and the temp agency) had put me in a job which officially hired me, and where I still am gratefully employed.

During my first year and a half of sobriety, I took the suggestion of avoiding romantic relationships, and I happily flew solo as I grew to know myself. Then, at eighteen months sober, I met the man who is now my husband, at an anniversary meeting. My first thought when I met him was "Wow! He loves being sober as much as I do!" After we had been together for three months, I started worrying about AIDS because I had used drugs intravenously. My new sober boyfriend had never used needles, nor had he been very promiscuous during his drinking, and I felt it was my responsibility to get tested. So in October of 1985, at twenty-two months sober, I tested positive for the AIDS virus. This means that I have the AIDS virus in my blood. In order to actually be defined as having AIDS, one has to develop any of several opportunistic infections that characterize the illness. So far, I haven't developed any of these infections. I've been lucky. When I first tested positive, my sober boyfriend left me, and I was sad but relieved. The last thing I wanted to do was to hurt this man that I had fallen in love with. On the night he left me, I was alone and scared, and I decided to finally talk about my situation at an open meeting. I figured that if everyone ran screaming out of the room, then I'd just have to find somewhere else to go and stay sober. To my surprise, after I poured out my heart, no one ran out of the room. Instead, I got so many hugs that I lost an earring! A few worried people even asked to talk to me outside, about their own situations. This made me realize that I had to be able to share about the AIDS situation at meetings if I needed to.

I was saddened to read "A Need for Accurate Info," in your February 1989 issue, about the AA who shared about having AIDS and all of a sudden people in his group were afraid to hold hands with him! Not only is AIDS not transmitted by casual contact such as hand-holding, but the person with AIDS is more at risk of catching illnesses from other people because of his or her compromised immune system. A friend of mine told me, "Don't drink, even if your bottom falls off. And when you're talking about AIDS, you're talking about bottoms falling off. So you have to be able to talk about it." I do talk about it at meetings when I need to. But I am often reminded of what my primary disease is: alcoholism. I must never forget that. My sober boyfriend came back to me two days after he left me, and I was so surprised! He said, "When I was drinking, I used to run away from everything, and now, I feel like it would be wrong for me to run away from this situation." We took it a day at a time, and we went on a quest for information about AIDS. This process was painfully slow, and gradually we worked out how we wanted to live our lives together, sexually and spiritually. We had to make some tough decisions that only God could help us with. We've been together ever since.

There have been other difficult choices to make. During my second and third years of sobriety, I was able to buy a new synthesizer and I was invited to play in a sober band. I joyfully discovered that I could play sober even better than I could when I had been drinking! But this band of sober friends had ambitions to take their act on the road, and I felt hesitant about pursuing the music business professionally again.

After all, I had a good job, a solid relationship, and I was also involved with the 30th International Conference of Young People in AA in Boston (ICYPAA), and the Massachusetts State Conference of Young People in AA (MSCYPAA). I knew in my heart if I wanted to do them justice, I would have to be totally committed to them. Choices in sobriety! It was during this time of indecision in my life that my ex-boyfriend guitar player died of AIDS, just over a year after I tested positive. Because I was sober, I was able to be of some help to his family. I was able to say goodbye to him before he died. Because of the Steps, I had already made my amends to him, and what struck me as I saw him dying in the hospital, was how little time he had left to make peace. I had my whole sobriety to make peace, and I will never forget the look on his face when I squeezed his hand and told him to "just keep talking about it." He was trying so hard to make amends and he had so little time to do it!

When my friend died, he took a part of me with him. I just didn't feel like playing music anymore, and it broke my heart. I left this sober band a few months later, and I focused my priorities on my relationship, my job, ICYPAA, and MSCYPAA. I realized that the main reason I had wanted to be in a band in the first place was to be part of a team that accomplished something wonderful. Being involved with the 30th ICYPAA in Boston in 1987, and being a co-chair of the third MSCYPAA was just as fulfilling; I was part of a team that was accomplishing something miraculous!

So here I am at just over five years sober, and I am watching in amazement as the Promises come true for me in my sobriety! My sober boyfriend and I were married last September, and our wedding brought my whole family together for the very first time. My family loves me and believes in me, and my husband's family has accepted me with love. I have a good job with great benefits and very supportive workmates. My health is still good, but I have to work very hard to stay healthy. I have been changing and improving my diet, my husband and I quit smoking over two years ago, we took up jogging last year, and I started a meditation class so I can better practice the Eleventh Step. I have a working relationship with a doctor I trust, and I participate in my treatment for the virus; I am not a passive patient, but an aggressive one. I share with my doctor about alcoholism and recovery, and we're learning a lot from each other! If it wasn't for AA, I would never have had the will nor the awareness to do the work I need to do to stay healthy and keep improving the quality of my life. Testing positive for the AIDS virus has also taught me how to work the Twelve Steps on a difficult situation. Because of the stigma attached to AIDS, and because of the uncertainty involved with having the virus, all my alcoholic character defects can become more extreme. I have to work very hard to constantly determine what is what. Is the fear I feel just plain old alcoholic impending doom, or is it legitimate fear because of the AIDS virus? Am I feeling sorry for myself because no one can tell me whether I'll stay healthy or get sick, or am I realistically appraising my situation and trying to be prepared for whatever might happen? Is my fear of rejection based on AIDS paranoia, or is it just another garden-variety alcoholic character defect? I continue to move ahead and set goals for my future, reminding myself that I do not have a corner on the uncertainty market and that taking risks is a part of living. But what should I have faith in? That God will protect me and my husband from harm so that we can realize our dreams together, and that we will both stay sober no matter what if we keep on working our programs the way we are. If God can help us stay sober no matter what, then I can have faith that all will be well.

Sometimes I beat myself up because I'm not a more serene person. One might think that, because of my situation, I would have an outlook on life of "Don't worry, be happy, because all we have is one day at a time." I realize that I shouldn't waste precious energy that is better spent on healing myself, but I get angry in traffic just like the next guy. I get resentments over stupid things, I'm very impatient, and I am an obsessive-compulsive perfectionist. I worry about money and whose turn it is to cook dinner after a hard day at work. Sobriety has given me the blessing of an (almost) normal life and all of the stresses that go with it. It's hard trying to live a spiritual life in such a material world!

Fortunately, the AIDS issue does not consume my life; I still worry about stupid stuff all the time. Maybe that's how I know I'm going to be alright! I have realized that it doesn't really matter what the crisis is; there is no one crisis that is worse than another. Everyone's pain is their own, and all pain is relative to the person who is suffering. And all the same rules apply to any crisis in sobriety: just don't drink, no matter what! Then the quality of our lives will continue to improve, and our crises will assume a proper proportion in our lives, so that we can live our lives to the fullest – no matter what our destiny may be, one day at a time.

Anonymous
Boston, Massachusetts
October 1989

In the Palm of My Hand

I saw a man wasted on the sidewalk the other day. As people hurried past with their eyes focused anywhere but on his wrecked body, I thought: That's me in those dirty clothes, in those busted shoes, in that state of hopelessness.

Some days it wouldn't take much, believe me – a slip in my recovery program, an imperceptible shift in my emotions or attitude, and – presto chango! – I'm no longer a well-respected professional, husband and father, a young up-and-comer, but an alcoholic, once again in full, seething insanity.

I have two lifelines clearly marked on the palm of my hand. My wife noticed them years ago. Now I know why: I've been given a choice between two very different paths in life. The first time I took a drink, at the age of fourteen, it was as if the world opened up and whispered in my ear: You've finally found something that makes you feel good inside and out. I don't think I sensed that afternoon that I had just put myself on a new life path, a path that would lead me to hospital emergency rooms, jails, and countless lonely motel rooms where I would spend terrifying hours of inexplicable self-loathing. Only another alcoholic truly knows that variety of soul-breaking desperation — to know that you are completely powerless over almost every aspect of your life, to accept the fact that you have surrendered to booze, that you somehow ended up on this dark path rather than the one you imagined for yourself as an eager young boy or girl.

People who don't personally know an alcoholic rarely have any sort of compassion or sympathy for those who refuse help or spend a lifetime in and out of rehab centers. And I don't blame them. The active alcoholic is about as pretty as a six-car pileup on a freeway on Friday night. We always "fall off the wagon" at the worst possible moments; we break promises as easily as we tell lies; we steal money from our kids' piggy banks in order to keep the high going so we don't have to face the reality of our situation. And the ironic thing is, the longer we continue, the more guilt and shame we pile on our already overwhelming load. So we drink more to wash it all away.

But everything that goes up must come down. Everybody hits bottom sooner or later. Maybe they live through it, maybe they die. It's a coin toss. I've had friends die in lonely motel rooms or at the bottoms of lakes or by their own hand. My personal bottom hit me in the face in January 2002. My maniacal on-again, off-again drinking finally escalated to a blackout and waking up in a jail cell again.

But something was different this time. Call it a vision or a spiritual experience, but I woke that morning with a very clear image in my mind of a police officer knocking on my front door to tell my four-year-old daughter that her daddy wouldn't be coming home again. I stood up in the cell and truly understood for the first time in my life that I was the only person I had been deceiving with my false recoveries and false admissions of defeat. It was time to get honest, or die.

Recovery isn't easy. My mind is like a trap, and I have to be ever watchful of dark moods and self-pity, my failure to be grateful. I don't understand why I've been saved from myself so many, many times: broken bones, crashes, falls, fights, blackouts spent wandering strange city streets. I don't understand why the man I saw in the street the other day is still where he is, and I am where I am. Doctor, lawyer, cop, steel-worker, street person — every alcoholic is exactly the same. I'm just one of the lucky ones I guess.

Heck, I'm a walking miracle. And I'm glad to be on a different path today.

Chris F.
Ottawa, Ontario
March 2004

Sober Shoelaces

When I arrived in AA, one of the first things I had to do was buy shoes. All I had were flip-flops, and Reading, Pennsylvania, where I lived then, was cold in the winter. I'd never owned a pair of high-tops, so my grandmother sent me a pair. I thought it would be cool to have two-colored laces which were the style then. But I couldn't lace them up. Two women in the halfway house helped me put the laces in the shoes. Then I went to tie them. It took me a long time, way longer than it should have for someone in her early twenties. But the girls at the halfway house just laughed and encouraged me until I finally got it. I still laugh when I think about it today.

I also celebrated my first sober New Year's Eve at the halfway house at a party of about 500. I've been to larger AA functions over the years, but nothing compares to that party when I was alive and sober, had plenty of food to eat, and had a roof over my head. I was grateful just to be alive. I felt part of AA.

Heather S.
Manteno, Illinois
January 2002

A Tough Pull

I am twelve years sober and thirty-one years old, so most of my adult life has been spent in recovery. Over the years, life has had its ups and downs but drinking has not yet been an option and with God's help, one day at a time, it never will. Two years ago I was a reservist flying medical air evacuation missions from Bosnia to Germany. On my return to the States, I decided to end my nomadic lifestyle. Little did I realize how dramatic – and traumatic – that would be.

I began dating and fell madly in love. I got a good job and felt my life was really on track, that I was being rewarded for a life well lived. I had forgotten the old saying that "everything we have is on loan from God." The first argument I had with my girlfriend was our last. Two weeks later I was involved in a head-on car accident. Because of that, I lost my flight wings. Three weeks later, just before Christmas, I was downsized and lost my job. I spent the next four months unemployed and unemployable, receiving no wages or benefits.

Through all this I went to meetings and shared, trudging along on a path through the woods I called my trail of tears. I would go walking, cry, and ask God to take away the physical and emotional pain. I barely kept the house from foreclosure and when I was just getting back on my feet, almost a year to the day of the accident, my barn burned down. I wasn't insured and lost almost everything. Six months later a brush fire sparked the garage and I lost the rest.

It has been difficult for me to accept myself and some of my decisions. I always want to be a perfect superhuman. But I've done the best I can with the information available, even if it might not be someone else's best.

Since all this began, several friends in AA have gone back out to do research. Several will never return. I've had to realize all over again that my past sobriety is not a ticket to future sobriety. I have to pay that fare and make the decision to recover daily. I don't want the living hell I had when

I was drinking.

Recovery gives me hope for brighter days. I'd like to tell you that everything I've lost has been returned tenfold but I cannot. My loved one is still gone, my body still hurts, I'm still grounded, my possessions are still ashes, and my pockets are still empty, but I am also still sober. I know today who and what I am and what is important. It is easy to tell everyone how great recovery is when things are going your way; I guess my job is to tell you how great recovery is when it is a tough pull. Had it not been for a solid sponsor and friends in AA being a keel for me when I was adrift in despair, I don't know where I would be now. I know that the sun can't shine every day but if I can stand the rain, I'll see the sun again, if I stay sober.

Scott R.
Bennettville, Minnesota
December 1999

Growing Up in AA

W hen I first came to AA, I thought I was much too young to be an alcoholic. I still had some partying to do. But then I went back to drinking, and I thought I was going to lose my mind. I reached a bottom so low I knew there was no hope for me and that I was going to be miserable for the rest of my life. I had just accepted that fact when God intervened, and once again I found myself in an AA meeting. Only this time it was different. I listened to the similarities, not the differences. For the first time in my life, other people understood me. I didn't feel so alone.

At nineteen years old, I was not the youngest member in Alcoholics Anonymous — but I felt like it. I was a scared little girl, very intimidated by the older members of AA. I constantly got comments such as, "You're so lucky to be here at such a young age" or "You seem too young to be an alcoholic." I didn't think I had anything in common with those who were older, and it was very difficult for me to reach out because I felt looked down on because of my age.

But after listening to people share, I realized that alcohol doesn't care what gender, race, religion — or age — we are. Alcohol can get the best of us no matter who we are. I finally realized that if I wanted to stay sober, I had to get past this age thing.

I got a sponsor (who was older than I was) and started working the Steps. I wish I could say that I breezed through all twelve and that my life changed overnight, but it didn't happen that way. Instead, I worked only the Steps I absolutely needed to, and my life stayed insane. What eventually happened was that I reached another bottom.

It says in the Big Book that there will come a time when no human power will be able to stop us from taking a drink. This is true. I had the bottle in my hand. It was only by the grace of God I didn't have to take that drink. I put the bottle down and immediately called another member of the program and from that point on my life really started to change. I dove into the Steps wholeheartedly and did everything that was suggested. I've come to have a strong appreciation and respect for the Steps. They saved my life.

Today I am twenty-three years old and have celebrated four years of sobriety. My life is good. I still have problems and some facts of my life remain the same. What is different is the way I feel about myself. I can honestly say that I love myself.

I'm grateful to those who carried me through my early sobriety, and most of all I'm grateful that I got sober when I did.

Instead of thinking that being young is a handicap, I realize that I have my whole life ahead of me. I don't have to suffer for many years. I can enjoy the things life has to offer.

Now when someone makes the comment "You're lucky to be here so young," I can honestly say, "I know!" with a smile.

Karin A.
Sunnyvale, California
April 1995